MARY JANE WALKER

Mary Jane Walker is a writer of historically well-informed travel narratives that come with an autobiographical flavour. *Go Greenland* is the latest book in a long series.

Living in the Southern Hemisphere, Mary Jane was long fascinated by the lands of the North at the other end of the world.

With many pictures and maps and links to illustrated blog posts and videos, *Go Greenland* is a great introduction to a fascinating island!

Mary Jane has also won a bronze medal from IPPY (the Independent Publisher Book Awards) for her book *The Neglected North Island* (2020) and has been placed as a finalist in travel in two other competitions for two other books, *A Maverick New Zealand Way* and *Iran: Make Love Not War*.

Email: maryjanewalker@a-maverick.com
Facebook: www.facebook.com/amavericktraveller
Instagram: @a_maverick_traveller
Linkedin: Mary Jane Walker
Pinterest: amavericktraveller
TikTok: @amavericktraveller1
Twitter: @Mavericktravel0

a-maverick.com

MARY JANE WALKER

Published 2021 by Mary Jane Walker

A Maverick Traveller Ltd

PO BOX 44 146, Point Chevalier, Auckland 1246

NEW ZEALAND

a-maverick.com

ISBN-13:

978-0-473-58978-3 (softcover POD)

978-0-473-58980-6 (mobi)

978-0-473-58979-0 (epub)

978-0-473-58981-3 (digital audiobook).

© 2021 Mary Jane Walker. All rights reserved. Except for the purpose of fair reviewing, no part of this publication subject to copyright may be reproduced or transmitted in any form or by any means, electronic or mechanical, including photocopying, recording or any information storage and retrieval system, without prior written permission from the publisher.

Disclaimer

This book is a travel memoir, not an outdoors guide. Although the author and publisher have made every effort to ensure that the information in this book was correct at the time of publication, the author and publisher do not assume and hereby disclaim any liability to any party for any loss, damage, or disruption caused by errors or omissions, whether such errors or omissions result from negligence, accident, or any other cause. Some names have also been changed to disguise and protect certain individuals.

Notes on Images

All maps and aerial and satellite images have north at the top unless otherwise stated. All photographs in the book are the property of Mary Jane Walker unless otherwise credited.

Covers and Fonts

Front cover and spine fonts are Impact Condensed. The interior text is typeset primarily in Garamond.

A Note on Maps and Images

If you have a copy of this book in which the images are printed in black and white, or if you have a reader with a black-and-white screen, you can see all of the images in this book that were originally in colour in full colour, and all of the images including chapter-specific maps generally at higher resolution, by going to the blog posts linked at the end of each chapter.

In fact, these blog posts will generally contain more images and other visual material than appears in the book.

Unless noted or indicated otherwise, all maps, aerial photos and satellite images are shown with north at the top.

Readers are in every case urged to make use of original maps (often zoomable if online) and guides when in the outdoors; the maps and aerial/satellite images shown in this book are purely for illustration.

For a literally more all-round perspective, you might also wish to look at some of localities I describe in the 3D view on Google Earth.

MARY JANE WALKER

Contents

Front Matter

Introduction *1*

The Lands of the Bear and those who have shared them *7*

Travel Tips for Greenland *9*

The Inuit of the Greenland seas *17*

The Rise and Fall of Viking Greenland: A non-fishy tale *21*

Arriving in Greenland! *29*

A Global Warming Frontline *39*

Cultures on Display *45*

One National Park, but many Hiking Trails *53*

Down to the Green Southwest *57*

Roaming to Igaliku *67*

Knud Rasmussen and the Origins of the Greenland Inuit *75*

The Regular but Intrepid Voyage of the Sarfaq Ittuk *79*

Ilulissat and the Huskies – And Greenland's biggest Glacier that isn't there anymore *93*

Conclusion, and Epilogue *115*

Acknowledgements and Thanks..*117*

Other books by Mary Jane Walker...*119*

Introduction

GREENLAND is a huge Arctic island that straddles the North Atlantic Ocean, between America and Europe.

I had always wanted to go to Greenland after hearing tales of its Viking colonisation, its indigenous Inuit inhabitants, and the way that it is now a frontline of global warming, its amazing two-mile-thick icecap now melting.

The following map shows just how much of Greenland is covered by this incredible, second only to that of Antarctica, and shown shown here as pure white.

Map data ©2021 Google

Some areas around the coast are ice-free. That is how Greenland got its name, bestowed by Viking voyagers and coastal settlers who dwelt there for a time in the Middle Ages, since in many places the ice cannot be seen from the coast. But these coastal fringes are small in comparison to the total area of this great ice-island.

Although it is, indeed, a huge island, Greenland's size is often exaggerated in standard map projections. Here is different map, which gives a truer indication of the size and shape of Greenland, shown at the centre in green. Which is of course highly misleading as to the actual colour of most of the island, even if its size and shape are shown more accurately!

'Location of Greenland' by Cannormah, Orthographic projection, 18 March 2015, CC BY-SA 3.0

As you would expect of a land dominated by a two-mile-thick icecap, the landscapes of Greenland are often harsh, and it is beyond cold in the wilder parts. Colder than you could ever imagine and then colder still – it can be hard to breathe, and your legs ache with the effort it takes to trudge through the snow, especially when you're not used to it. Through it all I found beauty in the most unexpected places – the cold air biting my cheeks as I was rushed along the ice by a team of sled dogs, or the beauty of the slate grey skies that threatened to rain but never did, the sheer height of some of the icebergs that stealthily slid across the surface of the water – hiding animal and marine life above and below the sea.

The greenest parts are found on the southwest coast, where you can go 150 kilometres inland in places before you get to the ice-cap.

It is also along the southwest coast that most of Greenland's rather small population of 56,000 live, in a string of coastal towns.

Most of the Greenlanders are indigenous Inuit people, who also refer to Greenland as Kalallit Nunaat, the land of the Kalaallit, the largest group of Inuit on the island though not actually the only one.

Why go to Greenland? Well, partly because it is there. But also, for the unique Inuit culture, which is generally not so accessible otherwise. For the beauty of the mountains and fiords. For the aurora borealis, if you are there outside of midsummer, when the sun either never sets or hardly sets, depending on where you are.

And even for hiking. For instance, from Sisimiut, which is one of the greenest parts, you can hike 160 km (100 miles) inland to a much smaller town called Kangerlussuaq (next to the island's biggest airport, ironically) by way of the so-called Arctic Circle Trail, though most people do it the other way around.

And yet, when I say, 'most people', only about three hundred people a year do the Arctic Circle Trail. So that is another attraction of Greenland: that it is unspoilt.

Sisimiut and Kangerlussuaq are on the southwest coast. That is where most Greenlanders live, in a string of colourful towns that are regularly visited by a ship called the Sarfaq Ittuk. The towns of the southwest coast include the capital, Nuuk, which has more than 18,000 inhabitants. Sisimiut is the second biggest town, with a bit more than 5,000 inhabitants.

The green landscape of the southwest was colonised at one time by the Vikings. However, the Viking colonies gradually died out, for reasons that aren't very clear but probably had something to do with a natural deterioration of the climate. This was not a problem for the indigenous Inuit people, commonly but misleadingly known as Eskimos, who were far more adapted to living in the ice and snow, and for whom the southwest was almost balmy.

The Inuit make up the bulk of Greenland's population these days. Technically part of Denmark, Greenland is nevertheless highly autonomous and ruled mainly by its indigenous people, in much the same way that some tropical islands of the South Pacific are technically part of New Zealand but otherwise largely do their own thing. All of the placenames in Greenland are now in Greenlandic Inuit, though in old atlases they bear Danish names.

I saw replica villages of the Inuit, who otherwise now live mostly in the modern towns. And ruins and replica villages of the erstwhile Viking colonists as well.

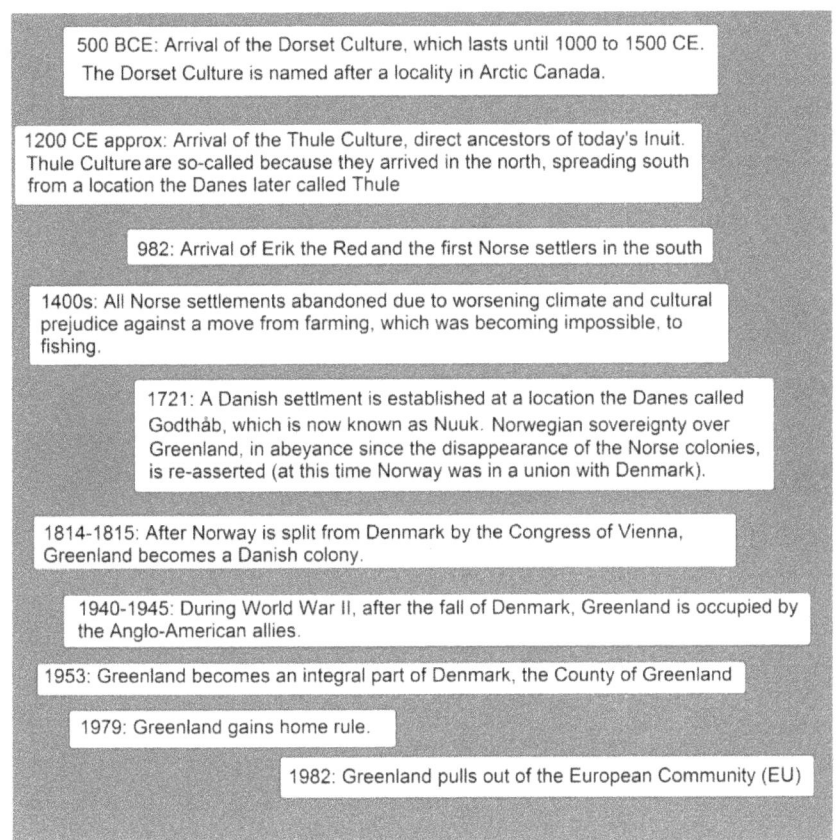

Some key dates in Greenland's history

I also learnt that the Vikings had established colonies in North America well before any other European people. Greenland had been an important stepping-stone for the Vikings, who island-hopped all the way from Scandinavia via the Faroes, Iceland and Greenland.

The effects of global warming are very evident in Greenland. Polar regions are warming faster than the rest of the world, and this has rained havoc on the Greenland people. The Greenlandic culture is suffering, and villages have had to relocate with some major lifestyle changes underway. No longer can they fish as they used to, in holes through the ice, as those holes are now seas and oceans.

What was the highlight of my trip? Well, I didn't do the Arctic Circle hike, unfortunately. But what I did especially enjoy was an even more unique experience, going dog sledding with a guide named Yush near Illulissat, the northernmost town that the Sarfaq Ittuk visits.

Illulissat, the former Jakobshavn, is also the site of the former Jakobshavn Glacier, at one time one of the largest in the world, but now almost all gone.

CHAPTER 1

The Lands of the Bear and those who have shared them

THE word Arctic comes from ancient Greek. It means the lands and seas 'of the bear', meaning that they lie under the northern polar constellation of Ursa Major, the Great Bear.

But the Arctic is full of living bears, too: of polar bears, and grizzly-type bears. So perhaps when we speak of the part of the world that belongs to the bear, that has a double significance.

Such were the lands of the bear which, due to extreme weather, dangerous animals and harsh landscapes, remain comparatively unpopulated to this day. Indigenous people make up much of the numbers in those areas where anyone lives at all.

I saw the impact of global warming for myself, most notably in Greenland. The fragile environment has become less dependable and that has meant a significant loss of traditions and ways of life.

The Inuit are the indigenous people of Greenland and of much of far-north Canada and Alaska as well. All Inuit people speak the same language, but in a continuum of dialects that stretches from Alaska to Greenland. The Greenlandic or Kalaallit Inuit have four main dialects, defined by the cardinal locations of north, south, east and west.

Large amounts of meat are consumed in the Arctic north, as edible plants do not grow easily there. The Inuit have some biological adaptations which means that eating large amounts of meat is not as unhealthy for them as it would be for most people.

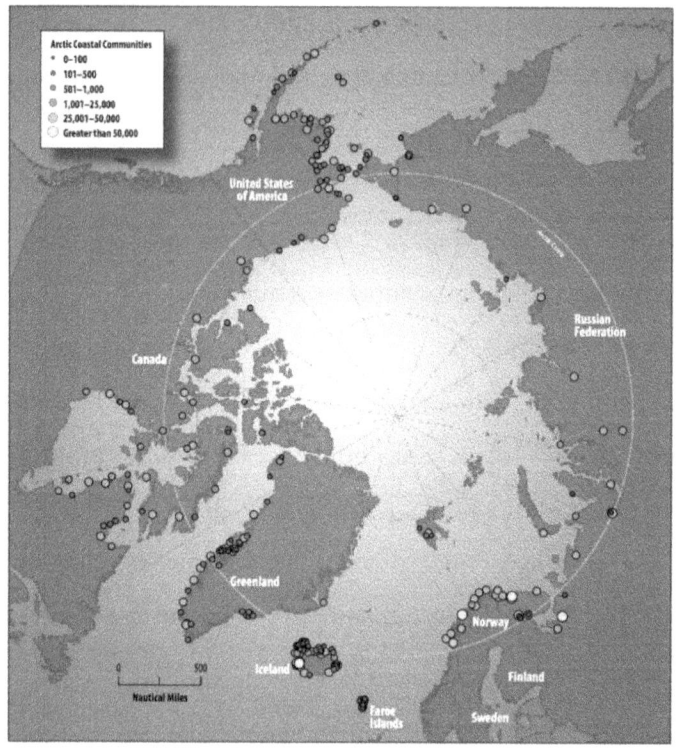

Arctic Circumpolar Coastal Human Population Distribution ca. 2009

Public domain image by Susie Harder for the Arctic Council
(via Wikimedia Commons)

For more, see:

a-maverick.com/blog/lands-bear

CHAPTER 2

Travel Tips for Greenland

ONE of the most important things about Greenland is that most areas outside the towns have no Internet. If you load up with apps, it pays to use apps that will work offline.

Useful apps for general Greenland navigation and wayfinding include **maps.me,** which works offline.

For checking the weather, **yr.no** and **windy.com** are useful but require internet access.

There are a number of apps on the Apple and Google app stores that you can bring up just by entering 'Greenland'. There is an information technology platform called Greenland, so you need to avoid those ones!

Titles include Greenland, Greenland Travel and Explore, Greenland Maps and Direction, Greenland Travel Apps and Search Hotels Price Greenland. As noted, the apps that will run offline will be the most useful. A lot of these don't get many reviews, so be sure to leave some!

One way to identify the ones that are about the physical place called Greenland is that they often bear the distinctive red and white Greenlandic flag, shown overleaf.

Public domain image of the Flag of Greenland by Jeffrey Connell (IceKarma), 9 October 2005, via Wikimedia Commons. This is purely for recognition purposes; there may be laws about how it is displayed.

When it comes to hiking in Greenland, the AllTrails app also has a great amount of detail on Greenland's hiking trails, and on its regions as well. AllTrails Pro allows offline downloads.

As to how you get to Greenland, you either get there by cruise ship, or by plane from Iceland or Denmark. Air Greenland flies directly from Denmark. IcelandAir flies to Iceland from a number of destinations. You can then carry on to Greenland via Air Greenland and AirIceland.

The indigenous Inuit language Kalaallisut is the most widely spoken language, though many people also speak Danish and English. It is not difficult for an English-speaker to get around, at least so long as you stick to the towns and the touristy parts of the country.

There are few roads, but many airports, in Greenland. The biggest airport in Greenland, Kangerlussuaq, is actually in an out of the way place, though handy if you are embarking on the Arctic Circle Trail, which is one of the best known of several major hiking trails in Greenland. (For more on hiking trails, see Chapter 8.)

The other airport capable of handling large aircraft is Narsarsuaq, closer to centres of population in the south. In general, as there are so many airports and external and internal route, it pays to coordinate your activities with flights served by Air Greenland and AirIceland.

Both of these airports were built by the Americans in World War II, Kangerlussuaq in 1941 and Narsarsuaq in 1942. At that time, Greenland had become an American protectorate in order to keep the Nazis from landing on the island. After World War II, Greenland reverted to Danish control, eventually gaining autonomy but never becoming fully independent.

Though Narsarsuaq and Kangerlussuaq are now civilian airports, the island continues to host an important American facility called Thule Air Base, which was was founded in the early 1950s in Greenland's remote far north at a spot known as Pituffik in Greenlandic. Thule is the old colonial Danish name for the locality, a name that survives in the name of the American air base though it is not otherwise officially used in Greenland anymore.

Only 947 miles or 1,515 km from the North Pole, Thule/Pituffik is definitely off the beaten tourist track, but Air Greenland does fly there occasionally in order to serve local indigenous communities, the base itself, and the odd occasional scientist or explorer. You can ride on one of the flights to Thule, though most people not associated with the base or with the local community will need a permit to get off the plane. Air Greenland's website has a page which deals with Thule base requirements.

The most active tourist destinations in Greenland, including the most popular hiking trails, are all in the south-west, which is the mildest part of the island, a region where the icecap is a long way inland in these parts, up to 150 km inland in places Rocks, meadows and even small areas of forest are thus able to warm up during long summer days to a reasonable temperature, sometimes even into the mid-twenties. Even the winters are mild by Arctic standards most of the time, at least so long as you are on the coast.

There is also another, perhaps more adventurous tourist destination on the south-east coast called Tasiilaq, served by the nearby Kulusuk Airport, which you get to by flying north-eastward across the icecap from Nuuk or, alternatively, by flying westward across the so-called Denmark or Greenland Strait from Reykjavík, Iceland.

(You can fly nonstop from Reykjavík to Nuuk, as well.)

From Tasiilaq, which has a population of about two thousand, it is possible to do maritime activities such as whale watching and kayaking, and also to go climbing and ice-cave exploring in the nearby Schweizerland region, also known as the Schweizerland Alps, which tower up to 3,383 metres (11,099 feet) at Mount Forel. The name has Swiss connotations, but of course the landscape is a lot harsher than at equivalent altitudes in Switzerland.

The ice cap is very close to the sea at Tasiilaq; which has an especially harsh climate as a result, including the piteraq ('that which attacks you'), a wind of supercooled and heavy air that plunges from the roof of icecap with extreme speed by the time it gets to Tasiilaq (up to 360 km/h or 200 mph) and bearing literally icy temperatures as well.

Common in East Greenland and another reason why most Greenlanders live in the west, the piteraq is technically known as a katabatic wind, a type of wind that is often visible as a sort of foggy waterfall of cold air descending down a mountainside, very much like the sort of thing you see if you leave the fridge door open on a humid day. Katabatic winds are common in mountain country, but usually not so extreme as in east Greenland. The only other place where such ultra-violent katabatic winds are encountered is Antarctica. So, Tasiilaq is for hardy souls.

Perhaps more intrepid still, further north on the east coast, is Scoresbysund, meaning Scoresby Sound, called the Kangertittivaq in Greenlandic. This is the world's largest system of branched fiords, penetrating inland by as much as 350 kilometres or 200 miles, in round and approximate terms, from the open sea. If the fiords of New Zealand's otherwise famous Fiordland National Park were that big, they would entirely cut the southern half of the South Island into a group of smaller islands!

For more on East Greenland, which seems to be the new adventure tourism frontier, see **Eastgreenland.com** and also a page about Kulusuk on the website of **VisitGreenland**.

There are many tour operators in Greenland, though it is hard to get a comprehensive list on one page. You can go on tours to places such as Scoresbysund, along with trips to other remote areas including the Schweizerland Alps, as well as trips up the south-west coast which include cruises on the Sarfaq Ittuk, a ferry that unites the communities of the south-west coast from Narsaq in the south to Ilulissat in the north, from which you can go even further on private tours to places such as Disko Island and onto the icecap.

But you don't have to be on an organised tour to board the Sarfaq Ittuk, which is operated as a public service. I sailed on the Sarfaq Ittuk on my own, and I talk all about that in Chapter Twelve.

The island's one national park is in the north-east, namely, North-East Greenland National Park. However, it seems that this area is so remote that the only people who go there are scientists.

Unless you are travelling at the height of summer, you might also get to see the Northern Lights (Aurora Borealis). You can get apps that will tell you whether the Northern Lights are active and even bring up an alert so that you get up to see them. These include **Northern Lights Aurora Forecast**, **My Aurora Forecast** and **Aurora Service Europe.**

The emergency number in Greenland is **112.**

Useful websites include the official tourism site, **visitgreenland.com**

Also useful is **guidetogreenland.com**

Most of the population has now been vaccinated against Covid-19, and tourism is starting up again as of the time of writing (September 2021).

When it comes to **medical matters,** you must have proper travel health insurance.

Apart from that, my loyal travel companion was my medical kit, which along with sticking plasters, bandages and scissors contained the diarrhoea stopper loperamide, some ciprofloxacin antibiotics, packets of Gastrolyte rehydration solution and Tramadol, Tiger Balm, Vaseline for dry skin, tea tree oil, iodine and bandages, and, finally, plain old paracetamol. Not exactly a romantic set-up, but realistic, nonetheless.

And also, be up to date with **vaccinations** before you go, **travel insurance** of every kind, and **travel advisories.**

For more, see:

a-maverick.com/blog/world-travel-tips

CHAPTER 3

The Inuit of the Greenland seas

THE INUIT tend to live close to coastal areas or spots good for fishing. Their way of life means they are dependent on marine animals for food, as well as on caribou.

Distribution of the language family to which Inuit belongs in the Americas and Greenland. The distribution in Canada and Greenland is exclusively Inuit.

Map by Ishwar, Wikimedia Commons, CC-BY-2.0

The Thule Culture, forerunners of the Inuit, originated in Alaska and migrated across Arctic Canada. About 1,000 years ago they advanced into Greenland. The Thule were more adept at making sophisticated tools for Arctic living than an earlier culture that lived in these parts, the Dorset Culture. Though technically a late stone age (Neolithic) culture, in the sense that they didn't make metals from scratch out of ore, the Thule culture practiced epi-metallurgy, meaning the use of metals that they found in the environment. Along with chert and flint, naturally occurring copper and meteoric iron were formed into cutting edges that made knives and harpoons more effective. The so-called 'copper Inuit' of northern Canada made use of naturally occurring copper, which can form a wicked edge like the points of copper carpet tacks. For their part, Greenland Inuit used iron from several large meteorites that crashed to earth near a future Danish settlement called Thule in the north of Greenland. The early Greenland Inuit radiated out from this area, assisted by their iron points, and was from that expansion that the expression 'Thule culture' arose.

The Inuit greeting in which they appear to touch noses was another point of interest for me. It is a lot like the New Zealand Māori hongi 11,500 kilometres away and the honi in Hawaii. I also saw a similar practice in the United Arab Emirates.

The Arctic was one of the last major areas in the world to be settled permanently. It is a common idea that the Inuit would have had some relation with the other native American groups further to the south, but DNA testing show they are quite distinct. Both populations resulted from migrations out of Siberia, but these took place many thousands of years apart.

The Inuit culture, like many other nomadic cultures is greatly dependent on the surrounding environment and nature. Shamanism is a major component of their way of life, cultural development and religions.

As they spread out through Arctic Canada and into Greenland, the Inuit diversified into sub-groups. The majority of the Greenland Inuit are known as Kalaallit, their language as Kalaallisut. This is the official spoken and written language of Greenland, often referred to in English as Greenlandic.

For more, see:

a-maverick.com/blog/inuit-greenland-seas

CHAPTER 4

The Rise and Fall of Viking Greenland: A non-fishy tale

WHEN the first Inuit settlers arrived in Greenland, packing their extensive survival toolkits, they would have come into contact with another iron-working civilisation, namely, the Norse. For settlements had already been founded in the south of Greenland by Erik the Red, a Norse explorer who was banished from Iceland for three years because of his involvement in a couple of murderous brawls.

During his exile, Erik discovered a new land, which he named Greenland because he wanted to back there with some fellow-colonists and settle down, away from disapproving Icelandic busybodies, and also because, as the old sagas frankly attest, Greenland also sounded a heck of a lot better than Iceland as a place to emigrate to.

This wasn't entirely a con on the Erik's part. The southwestern part of Greenland *is* green; it is reasonably temperate and though it is deforested today, in Erik's time it was actually wooded, with trees that were up to six metres high. The Norse founded two main colonies, one in the far southwest of Greenland, in the then-wooded area around today's Narsaq. This was known as the Eastern Settlement and probably contained about 4,000 people at its height. The other main one was called the Western Settlement, in the vicinity of today's Nuuk, which probably never got much above 1,000 people. There was also a smaller, and more ephemeral, Middle Settlement.

The main difference between the three settlements was latitude, not longitude. The Western Settlement was well to the north of the Eastern Settlement, which meant that it was colder and more marginal from a European standpoint. First the Middle Settlement, and then the Northern Settlement, were abandoned as the climate started to deteriorate at the end of the Middle Ages, in the early years of the episode known as the Little Ice Age. Finally, after centuries of occupation (and deforestation), the Eastern Settlement disappeared as well, during the early 1400s.

Ruins remain, such as the complex at an Eastern Settlement site which the Norse called Hvalsey ('Whale Island') and which the Inuit call Qaqortukulooq, near Qaqortoq in the far south of Greenland. These names mean 'big white' and 'white' respectively: researchers at the Greenland National Museum, which I visit in Chapter Seven, think that they refer to the walls of the Hvalsey Fjord Church, which were whitewashed when it was in use. The church is one of the most intact ruins in the Eastern Settlement, though it bears few traces of former decorative coatings these days.

So, the Norse left, and the Inuit moved in to occupy this part of Greenland. The Inuit, with their clever harpoons and other tools, were able to make use of marine sources of food like fish, bowhead whales, seals and other marine animals, whereas the Norse were never able to adapt to that sort of way of life and depended on European-style farming methods that the Little Ice Age rendered unviable.

Hvalsey Fjord Church, near Qaqortoq. Public domain image by 'Number 57', original upload date 3 August 2014, via Wikimedia Commons.

When it came to survival in the North, Viking technology might actually have lagged behind that of the 'stone age' Inuit in terms of ingeniousness and adaptation to purpose. But this certainly didn't mean that the Vikings weren't able to catch fish at all. Nor were they incapable of catching whales and other marine mammals, which were often classed as fish in those pre-scientific days, if they wanted to.

The reason why the Norse failed to make more use of marine resources as their farming failed is a little mysterious, given that

Scandinavians catch plenty of fish these days. However, one reason may be that the Viking-era Norse often kept slaves called thralls – the origin of our word 'enthrall' – and the thralls tended to be fed on fish while the higher-status free Vikings ate meat reared on land. As such, though they sailed about in boats, the Vikings remained landlubbers in their culinary tastes.

Thraldom was abolished in the Middle Ages, starting in Iceland in 1117 and everywhere in post-Viking society by the end of the 1300s, but it's likely that fish continued to be viewed as a low-status food for a time. So, it's possible that the free Greenland settlers decided that, if they were going to be reduced to eating fish to survive, they might as well pack it in! That's one big difference between the Norse Viking era and modern Scandinavians, who don't have any kind of taboo against eating fish.

It's a rather surprising difference, given how strongly modern Scandinavia is associated with the fishing industry and fish dishes.

The Viking fish-prejudice was widespread throughout the Germanic or Teutonic peoples, who very often made a distinction between themselves as eaters of meat and other supposedly lesser peoples who lived on fish. Thus the Germans, who expanded into territory occupied by Slavs in a similar or slightly later era than that of the Vikings, noted as a sign of the supposed inferiority of the Slavs that they tended to inhabit swampy areas and catch eels, erecting their villages on raised mounds of dry land. The landscapes of Eastern Europe, which are low-lying and often flooded, tended to favour such a way of life.

Borrowing hydraulic technology from their cousins the Dutch, who also inhabited a flooded landscape but had discovered how to pump out the water, the Germans drained many swampy areas and turned them into farmland and dairy flats, known in German as *Holländereien*. A practically identical story played out in the fens of East Anglia, inhabited by people who didn't like the Normans, and in colonial New Zealand as well, where the Māori caught eels in wetlands that the settlers saw as ideal for dairy conversion, if only they could be drained (and the Māori evicted).

Though it no longer exists in the original sense, the prejudice that linked the consumption of fish to an allegedly backward or low-status way of life, as opposed to respectable people who lived on the proceeds of sheep, beef and dairy farms, survives in the English language in the sense that we say of anything we don't like that it's 'a bit fishy'.

Fishing was a big industry in Norway by the 1400s. And later on, of course, we discovered the health benefits of cod liver oil and Omega-3s. But in the meantime, the old prejudice against fish seems to have lingered on in Greenland, where it probably also served to uphold a social distinction between Norse and Inuit. Norse Greenland, which could have prospered hugely from fishing but didn't, may thus have ended its days as a backwater clinging to the old, prejudiced ways while the rest of the world moved on, in ways that ultimately contributed to the colony's demise.

There was a similar situation in Iceland, though it didn't actually doom the colony. According to writings of the Icelandic economist Þráinn (Thráinn) Eggertsson, while the island's seas and fiords teemed with fish, post-Viking Icelandic society was dominated by its farmers.

The farmer dominated assembly called the Alþingi (or Althingi) passed new laws, after the emancipation of the thralls, to force labour to work on farms and not to do other things such as fishing, save on a small and amateur scale.

Farming was a bit less marginal in Iceland than in Greenland, and so the Icelanders managed to survive; though the country stagnated for several centuries, as did its population, which for an equivalent period of time did not greatly exceed fifty thousand. From the late Middle Ages on, other countries fished Icelandic waters on a commercial scale. The main harvesters of the fish were Iceland's more economically developed Norwegian and Danish overlords, of whom the last ruled the island as a dependency until the twentieth century.

This was an obviously colonial situation. The thinly populated margins of the Scandinavian world were often in a colonial position vis-à-vis Copenhagen, Stockholm and Oslo, and with Norway in a colonial position vis-à-vis Denmark, as if the system was like an onion, with layers. But if so, it was a colonial system that Iceland's local ruling class was quite happy to go along with. Colonialism is often a two-way street in this respect. A colonial system is seldom imposed entirely by force. It is more often a question of doing a deal with local elites, with the aim of making sure they won't do anything to stop outsiders harvesting the region's resources. The reason independence is often a disappointment is that the same local ruling class then takes over after independence, which is in that sense 'premature'. There has to be some kind of revolution in the economic structure or the political system first, if independence is to live up to expectations.

Not until the nineteenth century did Iceland get serious about developing its own fishing industry despite the abundance of fish in its waters. By the time that Iceland's independence came, a process that occurred in stages between 1918 and 1944, Iceland had already become more economically diversified, no longer in thrall to its farmers, and thus ready for independence.

Meanwhile, it seems clear that, whatever the motive, a form of agrarian chauvinism similar to the prejudice that had ruled Iceland in its centuries of stagnation had also doomed the more precarious Greenland colony.

For more, see:

a-maverick.com/blog/viking-greenland

CHAPTER 5

Arriving in Greenland!

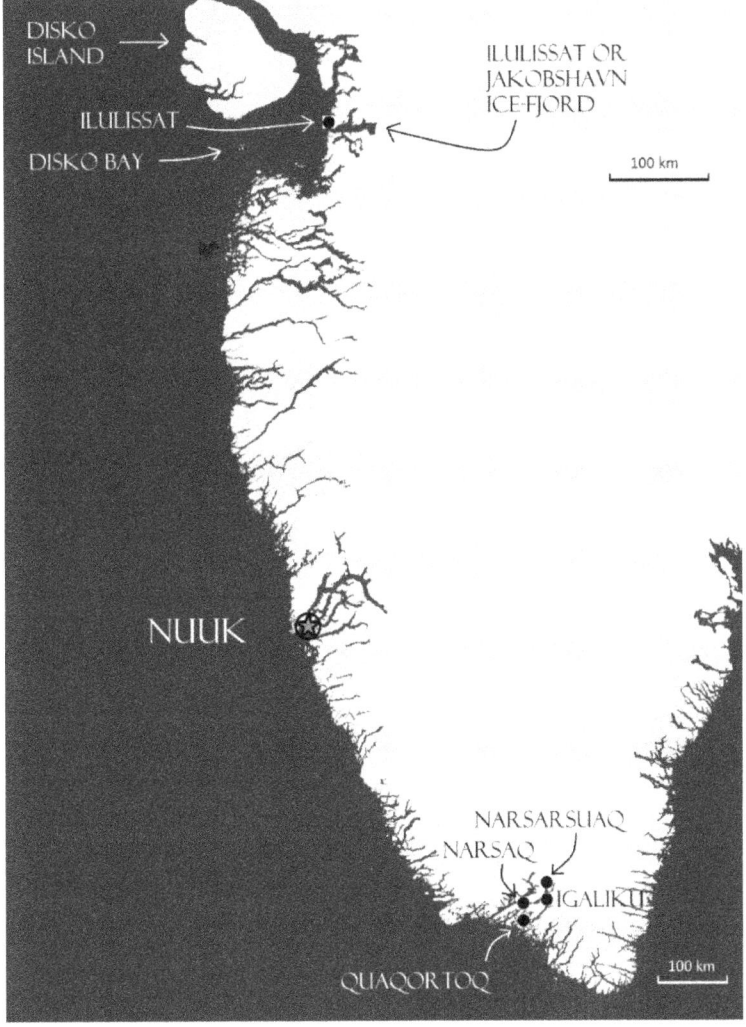

Greenland, showing some key towns and features mentioned in this book. Note that the scale differs from north to south. Visible fiords correspond roughly to the extent of ice-free surface.

GREENLAND conjures up images of ice, whales, catching fish and polar bears! I had always wanted to visit Greenland and learn more about the Inuit people and their way of life.

I knew that I had not chosen the best time to go. I was to arrive in April, which was still a cold time of the year and not yet the usual tourist season. But that didn't sway me at all: it just added to my excitement!

I did a great deal of reading before I went to Greenland and decided I wanted to see the fiords toward the north, which, unlike the ones in the south, would be frozen over: a unique experience! I read all the books by Lonely Planet and other authorities that I could and created my own itinerary from them. I would arrive at the capital city of Nuuk, travel to the southern town of Narsarsuaq and take a boat to Ilulissat, which is north of the Arctic Circle. It would be freezing to say the least. But then I live in Queenstown in New Zealand, a mountain town where the winters can be bitter, so I felt kind of prepared.

It was spring, so the days were getting longer and the nights shorter. I missed the Aurora Borealis, the northern lights, which are most visible in winter. But I could catch them next time and at least I did not have to put up with either the near-perpetual or even 24-hour-long winter darkness typical of polar regions, nor endless summer daylight either.

I got a flight to begin with from Copenhagen to the capital of Greenland, Nuuk, via a stopover in Iceland, which features in some of my other writings. The itinerary was pretty expensive though and cost me US $1790 return.

From Reyjkavík, Iceland, I flew across the Denmark (or Greenland) Strait to Kulusuk Airport on the east coast of Greenland, and then across the Greenland Icecap to the capital city of Nuuk on the west coast.

I had my face pressed up against the glass for most of the time. The water of the strait was slate grey, and it looked so cold. Every now and then I caught a glimpse of tiny islands and dots of white — icebergs. It was mostly a bland expanse of ocean, but I wasn't going to risk looking away, just in case I missed something!

Now, I tell you, Greenland was utterly amazing! Flying over snow-capped rugged hills and rocky mountains was just incredible. I was most glad to have a window seat!

At Kulusuk, and then at Nuuk, we flew in over harbours. Below, you could see ships going about their business and a smattering of buildings, more of them at Nuuk which is a sizeable town. I was blown away with the scenes below.

Getting off the planes, I was really amazed at just how rocky the landscape was. I could see the grey sky above that looked like it would rain at any moment. The planes themselves were quite interesting, specially built and designed to withstand rougher winds along with ice and snow.

At Nuuk, I found my accommodation via Lonely Planet at a place simply called 'Sam's Hostel'. It was only US $85 a night, which was a great price for Greenland, I thought (I had heard things can be quite expensive there).

I didn't expect to really enter a state of culture shock, but I did. Driving to my hostel gave me a very bleak view of the city. There were homeless people everywhere along the streets — something I did not expect to see, and it was so in your face. Unemployment rates were really high among the almost 18,000 people that call Nuuk home. What I found out that really surprised me is that even though Greenland is part of Denmark, out of the 57,000 people who live there 89% of them are Inuit.

This fact is reflected in the names of the towns, which used to have Danish names in most cases but now mostly have Inuit ones. For instance, in older atlases, Nuuk is referred to as Godthåb, and Ilulissat as Jakobshavn.

Many of Greenland's people want independence from Denmark, but then there is the other side to it too. Greenland is not profitable to Denmark, so it is almost like they are doing each other a favour by keeping this mutual relationship. Greenland is self-governing but depends on Denmark for income — so people do get by pretty well for a country where there is not much agriculture and only one single beekeeper in the whole country, at Narsarsuaq.

I did find that living costs and groceries were quite expensive in Greenland. The Greenlandic Krone was abandoned in favour of the Danish Krone in 2006, which drove the prices of food and everything up quite a fair bit. I suppose there is an adjustment period that they are still getting through.

As you can imagine there is a limit to the kinds of accommodation found in Greenland, but I was pleased to find Sam's Hostel, I really am a hostel kind of traveller. It is by far, my preferred style of accommodation!

I arrived and was greeted by a blonde-haired woman called Sylvia. When she learned it was my first time in Greenland, she insisted I get a special tour of Nuuk. I gratefully accepted, immediately feeling welcome in this very foreign setting. To be honest I found Nuuk to be a bit, well, bland, but the pops of colour on the exterior of the houses made up for it. There were no gardens and flowerbeds like there was at home, and a distinctive lack of greenery – so unlike New Zealand.

Sylvia was a missionary and a social worker living in Nuuk. She was married to the hostel receptionist, and they were originally from Denmark. I told her I had just visited Copenhagen, and she was interested to know what I thought of the city. They had lived in Copenhagen, and knew of the commune I had stayed in. One day, she told me they simply decided (with the help of Jesus) to move, so they sold everything they had and headed to Greenland.

They had come to do missionary work and help the Greenlandic people, who were suffering from homelessness, ill health and unemployment.

I saw the Nuuk Cathedral or the Church of Our Saviour that is located in an area known as 'old Nuuk'. It is but a simple weatherboard looking brownish red building: very modest but great to visit all the same. The area of old Nuuk was really interesting. Apparently, Sylvia told me, many houses still were without toilets and running water. It was a stark contrast to the newer areas and many Inuit people resided in old Nuuk. There seemed to be a not so invisible line of segregation here. Sylvia said she had met many of the local people who had had to move from smaller towns in the north and west because of the impacts of global warming.

Nuuk

Nuuk, with the cathedral, statue of Hans Egede, and Sylvia

Colourful Houses in Nuuk (top) and Ilulissat (bottom)
Both images by Patano, Wikimedia Commons, CC-BY-SA 3.0

Over-fishing was also becoming a huge problem and then unemployment on top of that – it just became impossible for them to make a living, so they moved here instead. Life in old Nuuk was relatively tough; Sylvia and her husband helped out where they could, even investing their spare time in local soup kitchen.

There is evidence of older churches further down the coast in an area settled by Erik Thorvaldsson or Erik the Red, a Norwegian Viking. Erik is mentioned in the Icelandic and Viking sagas for creating the first settlement in Greenland. Whether or not this is accurate, there are some amazing remains still there. Erik's son Leif, who went on to lead the first known European expedition to America, succeeded Erik as chieftain of the area. Leif also brought Christianity to Greenland. While Erik refused and discouraged the religion, Leif's mother quickly adopted it, sponsoring the construction of a church named after her, 'Thjóðhild's Church'.

It was not a touristy tour. It was a realistic tour I'd like to call it – one where I got to actually see both sides to a city and a country. There was a blizzard as well while I was being shown around, which made everything seem a lot bleaker than it usually was; snow and wind were coming in from all directions. I could see why mental health was becoming a big issue here too. Imagine a world full of grey most of the year round, with the only colour the prettified-up houses.

For more, see:

a-maverick.com/blog/arriving-greenland

CHAPTER 6

A Global Warming Frontline

PERHAPS you've seen Al Gore's 2006 documentary *An Inconvenient Truth,* with its memorable images of deep blue rivers of meltwater flowing across the Greenland icecap before plunging into terrifying holes that bring to mind Coleridge's line about how 'Alph the sacred river ran / Though caverns measureless to man'.

Where this meltwater goes, nobody knows, or not in detail at any rate. But we do know that a lot of it eventually percolates into the ocean, where it contributes to sea-level rise.

Global warming is a very controversial topic and the fact that I saw the effect of the warming ocean and rising sea levels for myself made me very conscious of it. There are islands like Kiribati which are suffering massive land loss every year – at an incredible rate actually. It's the warming of the Arctic that cause more icebergs and ice sheets to melt and massive amounts of water pour into the ocean causing the levels around the world to rise. I saw a documentary where the prime minister of the Pacific tropical islands of Kiribati went to the Arctic to see where all the water was coming from – he was convinced of global warming and was urging people to keep in mind the impacts of climate change. For him and his people it was very real!

Although global temperatures have warmed by only just over a degree Celsius since the Industrial Revolution, so far, the warming is more concentrated in Arctic and Antarctic latitudes, and Greenland is now between two and four degrees Celsius warmer than it used to be in the mid-nineteenth century. Winters are in places up to ten degrees warmer, which has implications for the generation of sea ice. Overall, this warming has had very real and visible effects including the shrinkage of Arctic Sea ice and the almost total disappearance of the Jakobshavn Glacier near Ilulissat, a famous glacier which used to be one of the largest in the Arctic.

Where the Jakobshavn Glacier used to be in 1850, there is now just a huge fjord extending more than 50 kilometres inland. This is a very dramatic event to have happened on such a short geological timescale and it happened, partly, because of a phenomenon called ice-cliff instability. Normally, the ice of Greenland and Antarctica taper down to the sea, or to dry land short of the sea. Actual ice cliffs much more than 100 metres high aren't stable and collapse under their own weight, creating another cliff behind – and so on.

So, the whole icecap doesn't have to melt right *where it is,* in order to wind up in the sea as additional water promoting sea level rise. All that's required is for the tapering edges to melt away, and then the thick ice of the interior will start falling down around the edges, in great chunks. The fallen ice will help to prop up the ice cliff behind, just like the tapering ice that used to be there in the same place. But if the broken ice falls into an area that is now open sea, the sea will quickly wash the fallen and broken ice away, exposing a new, bare, cliff face to crumble some more. This is a significant worry wherever the bedrock level under the ice cap is below sea level – which is actually the case for much of Greenland and

Antarctica. Thus, a massive deep-frozen icecap could collapse quite quickly and be replaced by open sea, something that is also called the Jakobshavn effect.

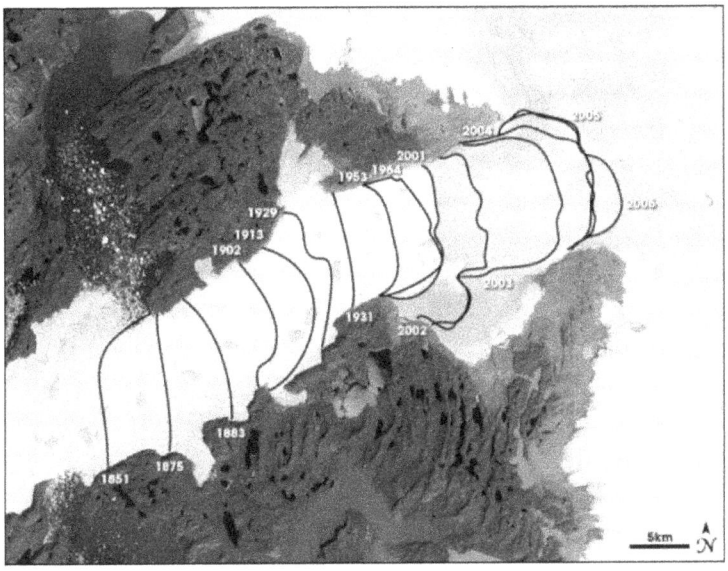

The Jakobshavn Effect. The roughly 50-kilometre retreat of the Jakobshavn Glacier between 1850 and 2006 (it's crumbled a bit more since then and the ice cliff collapse is now biting into the ice-cap proper).

Public domain image from the NASA Earth Observatory, 2007, via Wikimedia Commons.

Along with the Jakobshavn effect, in 2012, melting ice was recorded almost everywhere over the Greenland ice sheet in mid-summer, that year. Normally, melting of this kind is only seen around the tapering edges of the ice sheet and not in the thick, deep-frozen interior. In other words, the icecap is threatened not only by melting at the edges and subsequent crumbling due to the Jakobshavn effect, but also by actual melting-in-place. When these effects are combined with various other phenomena that also undermine the ice sheet, such as the lubrication of the bottom and cracking of the ice caused by the weight of the plunging water (denser than the ice, of course, and capable of acting like a wedge in a crevasse), it leads to a worrying picture. Estimates of how quickly the Greenland ice cap could break up melt in the face of sustained warm temperatures are constantly being revised in the more-quickly direction.

More recently, in 2021, rain was recorded even at the highest point on the Greenland icecap, something that has never been seen before. Of course, rain has a powerful melting effect on ice and snow. Even if rain only melts the snow on top, it exposes the transparent ice below, which often looks deep blue or black, and which absorbs the sun's rays in much the same way that open seawater does.

I did see the evidence of ice melt in exhibitions in several of the museums I visited around Greenland. The ice melt is guessed at being in the trillions of tonnes every year. There was concern expressed by the locals when I asked them about it – it was more that there was not only a loss of land but also cultural practices like Arctic fishing and hunting. At the museum in Nuuk I would visit the next day, I saw how the Inuit would cut holes in the ice and put down a rod with 15 hooks attached to it. Fish used to be abundant in Greenland's waters, and no one went hungry after a fishing trip. More often than not, now, they don't catch anything.

For more, see:

a-maverick.com/blog/global-warming-frontline

CHAPTER 7

Cultures on Display

I DID get to see the one and only shopping mall in Greenland. It was called the 'Nuuk Centre' and was quite a modern building, opened for shopping in 2012. We also passed by Katuaq, a grand building that was used as cultural centre in the heart of the city and not far from the Hans Egede Church.

The Hans Egede Church was named after a Lutheran missionary. He founded Greenland's capital Nuuk (as Godthåb) in the 1700s and was credited as re-establishing friendly relations with local Inuit, after a fractured relationship with Denmark. The church was in commemoration of his work, and he is well-known as the apostle of Greenland.

I heard a funny story about Egede. When he began working with the Inuit people and preaching to them, he ran into a classic example of cultural differences. When first reciting the line from the Lord's Prayer, 'Give us this day our daily bread' the local Inuit had no idea what bread was – it was not in their diet. Hans had to translate the saying to, 'Give us this day our daily seal'!

There were a few statues to Hans Egede around Nuuk, and I noted with surprise that there had also been a statue of him outside Frederik's Church in Copenhagen: the one with the marvellous dome. I suppose that ties in with Hans going to university there and living in Copenhagen.

I headed to the National Museum of Greenland in Nuuk, which had an exhibition on about the Inuit people and their traditional ways of life. It covered everything from 4,500 BCE until modern times and was beyond interesting. It wasn't a massive building or anything, but they sure had a lot of information.

The clothing was amazing. it began as fur and skins sewn together to form the iconic fur hood jacket that many people associate with the Arctic. The Inuit gave us the word 'Annoraq' (Anorak in Canadian Inuit), and 'parka', which is a traditional fur lined jacket used by the Inuit peoples across the arctic. They had to have been very skilled sewers, because they had to make sure the clothes didn't freeze and that they were watertight when they went out fishing.

So, it really was another example of their close relationship with, and respect for, the environment and animals they hunted. They used everything from an animal – it provided food, clothing, tools and more. I saw some of the very colourful traditional costumes that people in Western Greenland still wear today. I also saw an article about the crown princess Mary of Denmark and her husband crown prince Frederik, who both donned traditional outfits out of respect for the Greenlandic Inuit culture.

Greenlandic traditional clothing developed over time from fur and skins to become brighter in character once brightly coloured beads began to be imported from Europe. The women were particularly taken with the colourful beads, which are now a significant part of traditional Greenlandic clothing. The boots the women wore were another interesting item. Made usually from sealskin, the boots went all the way up to the mid-thigh and were then tied with string to hold them up. They were painted and decorated in a range of different colours, I thought them to be very trendy and they looked like something from the hippie era. Maybe that's where the inspiration for thigh-high boots came from!

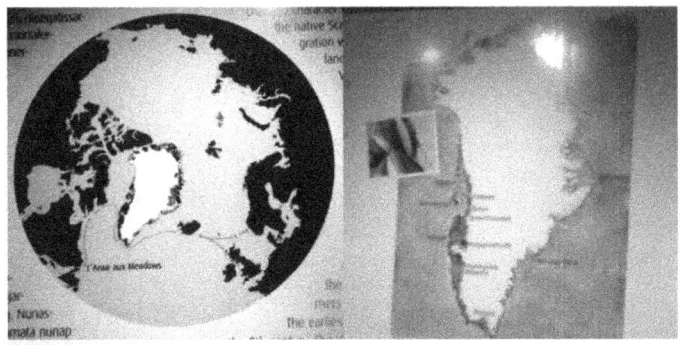

Nuuk Museum maps of Viking routes and the habitable parts of Greenland today, along with modern accommodation in Nuuk

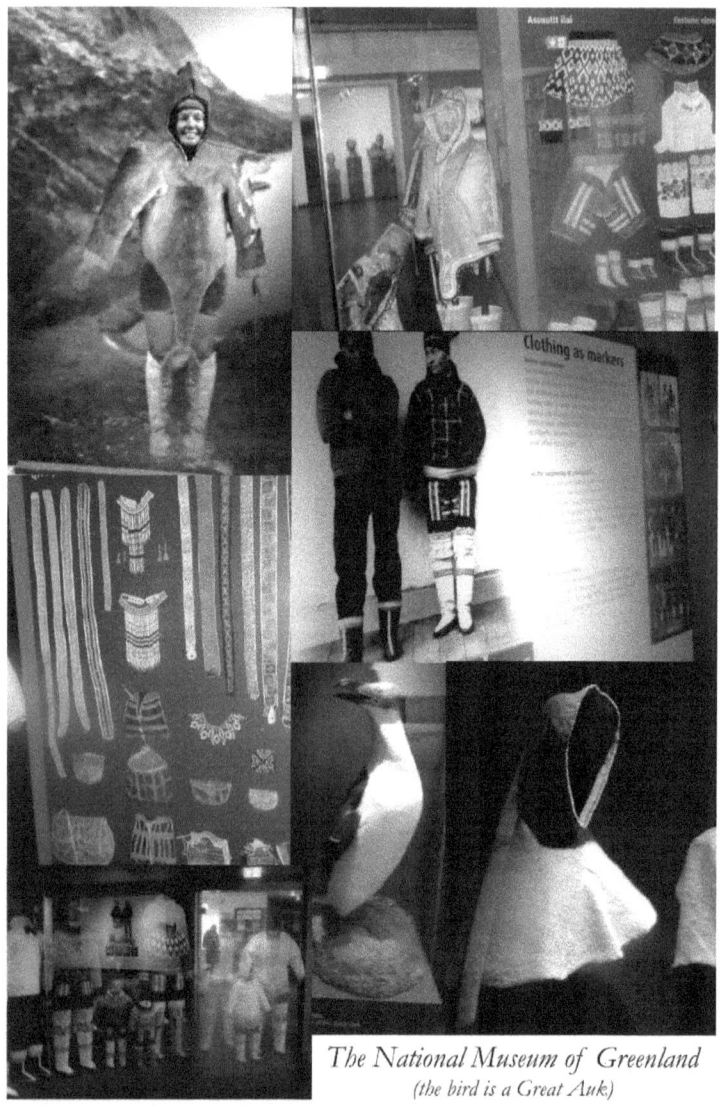

The National Museum of Greenland
(the bird is a Great Auk)

The exhibition that sparked my interest was the Thule culture, the forerunners of the Inuit. Because of the cold and freezing temperatures, there were a lot of mummified bodies that had been found and preserved in the museum. There were two main cultures who resided in Greenland before the Thule culture. They disappeared from Greenland, and it is believed that simply the weather was too much. Even the Norse people left eventually because of the weather, abandoning the island until the 1700s. It was the Thule culture who developed many of the strategies and ways to manage life in the harsh environment. They developed the kayak, dog sledding and more advanced harpoons for whale hunting. Modern day Greenlandic Inuit are said to be very closely related to the Thule people.

I found it all fascinating! I came all the way to Greenland, which I thought wouldn't have much of a history at all and found myself absorbed by ancient cultures and mummies in glass.

It was quite interesting the similarities and likeness to other cultures, particularly the other Inuit in Canada and the Native American peoples. I saw an umiaq, a skin boat. It is literally a boat made from the skins of animals sewn together. Archaeologists had found one in the north of Greenland which they called the Pearyland Umiaq, and they reckon it was built around the 1400s, which was just incredible! The boat's origins are said to be from the Thule culture and just passed on down through generations, all the knowledge about how to make them so they were watertight. That's one thing I suppose was saddening: the loss of culture and traditions in many of the countries I visited and cultures I saw.

Another traditional mode of transport is the dog sled. No less than 82% of Greenland is ice cap. So, the whole dog sled thing was quite significant. There are no roads in a lot of places to connect villages, so people depend on other means of transport: which traditionally boiled down to a choice of boats in the water and dog sleds on the ice. Even well into the twentieth century the dog sled was important. There was epic case in 1925 in which diphtheria anti-toxin was heroically raced to Nome, Alaska through the depths of the northern winter by teams of dog sledders, in fifty-below conditions, to combat a growing epidemic among the children of the town. But that was really the last hurrah of the dog sled. Within a decade any such crisis would have been handled by plane or – a little later still, and if the distances weren't so great – by snowmobile. These days, dog sleds exist only for old times' sake.

I spent a good part of my day wandering around the museum, making a point to read every single article and information board around the place. I found all the staff very polite and was surprised to find out that a lot of Greenlandic people have lost the local language. Many can only speak English or Danish, I think that is absolutely outrageous! Afterwards I wandered around the town a bit more, had a coffee and talked to a few of the locals who were sitting there too. I was surprised to meet a few people from Asia, even Thailand and the Philippines. However, most people seemed to be native Greenlandic people or Danes from Denmark as well as people from other parts of Scandinavia. I learned also that they take it very offensively when people use the term Eskimo, as common as it might be in Alaska.

Eskimo is apparently a word that used to be used by native Americans for their Arctic neighbours, with a meaning that is now unclear. Those who think it means 'eaters of raw meat' (true enough on occasion, traditionally speaking) are likely to take offence; though it could also mean 'wearers of snowshoes', which doesn't sound like any kind of an insult. In Greenland and in Canada, anyone who might once have been called an Eskimo is actually an Inuit. So, in those countries people now think the word Eskimo is dated and colonial. On the other hand, the word Eskimo is still used in Alaska as in that state there are two groups of indigenous people with an Inuit-like lifestyle, the Inuit themselves and the Yup'ik, members of an ethnic group that is related to the Inuit but not quite the same, and whose members live on both sides of the Bering straits whereas the Inuit are generally further east. In Alaska, the word Eskimo is used to refer to both Inuit and Yup'ik together.

In Nuuk, I also got to talking to a few of the locals about global warming; and that got me on to reading books about it. I found a book the Canadian Inuit people released in 2016, called "The Caribou taste different now," which was a reflection of how global warming had affected their lifestyles and diets. That was quite an eye-opener.

Traditionally the Inuit people had two homes – somewhat similar to the Sámi people, who moved around with the herds and seasons and had multiple homes as well. In the case of the Inuit there were generally two types of houses: a summer and winter version. The summer one looks similar to a native American tipi or a Sámi lavvu – a conical dwelling with a frame made from driftwood and antlers, which is then covered in skin, with a hole in the top for ventilation. The winter house is the more distinctive igloo, a snow house made out of blocks of compressed snow and ice that are cut into shape.

The central theme of the museum seemed to be the unity of the Inuit and their relatives across the Arctic from Siberia to Canada and Greenland. All in all, even though they are separated by distance, their cultural identities and characteristics are similar.

Art and music are also things that I am very interested in and familiar with, from cultures I have discovered all over the world. So, it was interesting to see such diversity in the development of traditional arts, crafts and music in the Inuit peoples. Song, poetry and stories seemed to be bound up with most of the Inuit art forms. Drumming and dancing as well as throat singing – which is very similar to the Native American chanting – were all part of the exhibition as well. The Greenland National Museum at Nuuk was incredible: well worth visiting.

There was a wealth of information, and it was perfect to see everything up close! I was glad I had got to see this slice of history and was quite keen to visit other museums and cultural sites.

For more, see:

a-maverick.com/blog/cultures-on-display

CHAPTER 8

One National Park, but many Hiking Trails

North-East Greenland National Park
Black lines are local government boundaries, park is in red

Map by NordNordWest, Wikimedia Commons, CC BY SA 3.0.

THERE is only one National Park in Greenland. That sparked my curiosity. It's called the North-East Greenland National Park and is a really wild place!

While Greenland is 82 per cent icecap, this still leaves huge areas that aren't covered in ice, even in the far north. Unfortunately, though, Northeast Greenland National Park is only a scientific reserve. The only tourism in this area takes place in and around the vast, branched fjord system of the Scoresbysund or Kangertittivaq, which overlaps the southeastern corner of the national park.

All the same, there are plenty of other places to go hiking in Greenland!

Hiking is my forte. I love hiking and being outdoors in general. I had thought to myself, what better a place to go for hikes than in Greenland!

I had done a fair amount of reading and research into hiking in Greenland. I was a bit disappointed to see that most of it needs to be done in their short and sweet summertime. Otherwise, you risk doing it in freezing winter weather, though some outdoors experts go hiking even then.

The best-known route is the Arctic Circle Trail, a 160 kilometre walk through the glacier and alpine environments inland, between Kangerlussuaq, which is at the head of a long fjord and also the location of the Kangerlussuaq airport, and Sisimiut, which is on the main coast and one of the towns that the Sarfaq Ittuk coastal vessel stops off at (see Chapter Twelve).

Reading about the Arctic Circle Trail had me mesmerized, and also kicking myself. If only I had been just a fraction more organised to delay my trip by a month, I could have walked more of the trails. Then again, I might not have been able to go dog sledding on the frozen Ilulissat Icefjord, which I talk about further on in Chapter Thirteen. It would make sense to try and time a visit for the overlap of sledding and hiking seasons, if any.

A lot of people in online blogs and forums had suggested just making your own way, provided that you report where you are going to the authorities. You could do that quite easily in Greenland with all the wide-open uninhabited spaces. I learnt that in Greenland there is no privately-owned land. So, you could just walk here, there and anywhere: a hiker's dream!

Otherwise, there were a lot of trails around the glaciers that wove up the sides of small mountains and hills and across rocky, snow-smattered landscapes. If you are into hiking, like I am, you'd be drooling too.

You can book tours and everything too. I discovered there are even New Zealand hiking companies who operate guided walks across the Arctic. The Ilulissat Icefjord also had a number of trails around it, so I took note of that. It was definitely on my to-do list!

In Nuuk there were several hiking trails including up the mountains called Lille (little) Malene in Danish, or Quassussuaq, which is around 440 metres high, and Store (big) Malene in Danish, or Ukkusissat, which is around 775 metres high and generally requires a guide for safety. The lesser peak hosts Nuuk's skifield, Sisorarfiit, in winter, and makes for a pleasant hike past a mountain lake in the summertime. The greater peak has a very good view over the town of Nuuk and its coastal fiord, especially in the long summer twilight hours, a special experience which you will hardly get anywhere else that is otherwise reasonably accessible. I had thought about doing one or the other, but the weather just wasn't going to play ball, so I left the hiking until I got to Ilulissat.

It is also possible to hiking, via guided tours, on Disko Island north of Ilulissat, and up onto the Greenland Icecap.

Lastly, as I mentioned in Chapter Two, there are also hiking trails in the realm of East Greenland, also operated by tour companies. These include hikes up the Schweizerland Alps and in an area called Liverpool Land, adjacent to the Scoresbysund/Kangertittivaq.

For more, see:

a-maverick.com/blog/greenland-hiking-trails

CHAPTER 9

Down to the Green Southwest

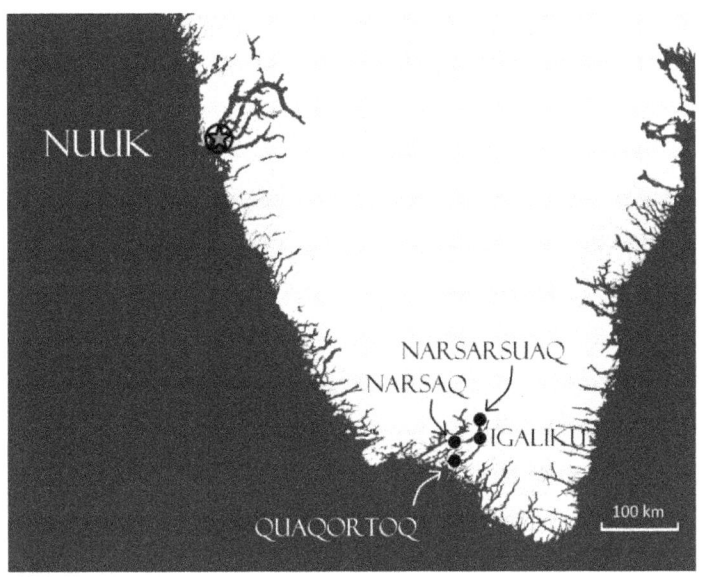

Greenland, from Nuuk down to the green southwest around Narsarsuaq. Visible fiords correspond roughly to extent of ice-free surface, which is comparatively abundant both around Nuuk and around the southwestern towns

THE next day, the thirtieth of April, I headed back to Nuuk Airport to catch a local flight down to southwest Greenland. It was snowy at the airport: the summer tourist season had still not yet arrived!

The name I was most familiar with down south was Narsarsuaq, though that only turned to be only the name of the airport.

Narsarsuaq is about an hour's flight south from Nuuk by local propellor planes, and is also on the west coast.

While the Inuit came from the frozen north, it was the southwestern area that was colonised by the Vikings who gave the island its otherwise misleading name of Greenland. For although it is only a small part of the whole island, the southwest is quite green in summer. There are even patches of forest in the southwest. The rest of Greenland is quite bare.

The southwest also has some farms, mainly focused on rearing sheep. Sheep farming is in some ways the last resort of the farmer in cold climates. As in the Shetlands and the Falklands and Norway, the South Island High Country of New Zealand and Wyoming, so, likewise, in the southwest of Greenland they run sheep.

The airport at Narsarsuaq was constructed by the Americans during World War II. During the war the small settlement was home to 4,000 people and included a hospital for wounded personnel. It was a strategically important location giving easy access to Europe. The Thule Air Base is another American military base that is still occupied and used in the very northwest of Greenland.

In 1959 the USA signed an agreement with Denmark to share the airport at Narsarsuaq, and both Icelandicair and Scandinavian Airline systems began flights to and from the airport. Icelandicair had the intention of creating a Narsarsuaq – Copenhagen route but because of the economy and lack of interest the route was never made available. Eruptions from nearby volcanoes in the area also didn't help the airport.

When I flew from Nuuk into Narsarsuaq it was really scenic, an eagle–eye view of the massive Tunulliarfik Fjord around Narsarsuaq. The flight I got was about lunchtime and as we approached the airport in the small plane, I was mesmerized by the deep green ocean with hundreds if not thousands of tiny icebergs floating along. I would liken it to flying over rural New Zealand's green fields dotted with white sheep – kind of.

In 2010 the Greenland census reported that Qaqortok had a bit over 3,000 permanent residents. For anywhere outside Nuuk, that is a lot by Greenland standards. "Permanent" means sticking out the winter: and it's that that separates the players from the stayers in Greenland. Nobody wants to be anywhere too remote when the big freeze-up comes. For instance, the permanent population of the Northeast Greenland National Park is precisely zero. Even the South Pole has more year-round inhabitants than that.

I wanted to visit this part of Greenland because not only did it have strong ties with local Inuit, but also, Erik the Red's settlement was near here. Erik the Red was the Viking explorer who founded the first European settlement in Greenland – the founding father. There was a museum to Erik the Red in the nearby town of Narsaq (permanent population 158); which I also confused with Narsarsuaq at first but is some distance away from the airport.

Directly across the waters of a narrow fjord from Narsaq is Qassiarsuq, where there is a sheep farm that tourists can visit, a statue of Leif Erikson and even a small plantation forest. There is also some natural forest in south-western Greenland, but it is some distance away and in a fairly remote area. It seems that there was more natural forest once, but the Vikings chopped quite a lot of it down and in view of the marginal conditions in this part of the world, the natural forest hasn't easily regrown.

Qassiarsuk with the sheep farm and statue of Leif Erikson

Qassiarsuq, with more sheep farm scenes and the Qassiarsuq Forest!

There are some quite famous church ruins here as well. The ruined, mediaeval Hvalsey Fjord Church near Qaqortok is believed to be the very first Christian church in Greenland.

This south-western corner of Greenland is sometimes jokingly referred to as the Greenland Riviera. It's also referred to as Erik the Red's land, mainly because this was the part of Greenland that Erik encouraged his fellow-Vikings to settle, forsaking the icier parts.

During the Viking era and the Middle Ages, the vagaries of currents and climate meant that the area was a little warmer than it would be over the next few centuries, until recently once more, which also meant that it could support a prosperous farming lifestyle. When the climate grew colder toward the end of the Middle Ages, the Vikings packed up and left. The last known record of their presence was recorded very early in the 1400s. After that the wind just whistled past the Hvalsey Fjord Church, century after century: quite sad, really. It's good that people have come back.

It was in Narsaq that I saw firsthand traditional Greenlandic culture for myself. Meat eating is a way of life in the Arctic – and there's no need for freezers either. Many Greenlandic Inuit store their meat under their houses in a basement-type space. I was told most meat is boiled, used in stews and soups. Anything they can catch is turned into an interesting main meal. Killer whale (orca), seabirds, wild duck, seals, polar bears: everything is used and turned into something most Westerners wouldn't even be brave enough to eat.

I was told about kiviak, a wintertime Inuit special. Little auk sea birds are stuffed inside a sealskin – beaks, feet, feathers and all – and then left to ferment for several months. The result looks like blackened roadkill. To be honest I was not brave enough to try it.

Most of these exotic fermented foods, so I'm told, end up smelling like a really stinky cheese or fermented tofu, which also smells like a really stinky cheese. As with stinky cheese, which at least doesn't look like roadkill, this is an acquired taste; you either love it or you hate it.

Apart from the risk of having the whole lot simply go rotten, the main danger with things like kiviak is botulism, which is normally kept at bay by encouraging an acidic fermentation process of the kind that also helps to create yogurt and sauerkraut. People have died from having kiviak improperly prepared, due to the loss of the traditional knowledge of how to get it right. And that's something else to think about.

There is only one beekeeping establishment in all of Greenland, at Narsarsuaq. They have something of a corner on the supply of honey in the country!

Seal meat hanging out to dry on St Lawrence Island, Alaska, 2014

Public domain image by Captain Budd Christman, NOAA Corps (USA), via Wikimedia Commons

I just found it so interesting that this was such an environmentally conscious land – I mean, yes, they are big meat eaters and, no, they don't eat baby seals. But they do eat and hunt whales and larger marine life because the by-products are all useful – the fat, the oil, the blubber, the skins – everything is useful!

That got me interested in the policies on hunting in Greenland and if there were any. The Greenlandic people are very well aware of overfishing and climate changes that affect the animal and sea life around the country.

Traditionally, the Greenlanders used polar bear skins in clothing, and they still consume its meat today. The polar bear is used in the official coat of arms of Greenland, symbolising its strength and importance to the people. The polar bears live in the very north of Greenland and along the western coasts; you can travel up there on tours during the summer to see them, although the polar bear is still considered a rare sight. The current law is that polar bears can be hunted but only under special circumstances. And, as tradition says, the whole animal and all its by-products must, as far as possible, be used and not wasted (surprisingly enough, the liver is poisonous).

The Soviet Union was the first to ban hunting of polar bears in 1956, Canada followed in 1968, and Norway in 1973. The USA, Soviet Union, Canada, Denmark (in charge of Greenland) and Norway (in charge of Svalbard/Spitzbergen) jointly concluded an Agreement on the Conservation of Polar Bears in 1973, which allows people to only hunt by traditional means and for traditional reasons. Iceland didn't sign this treaty, as polar bears are not native to Iceland and on the odd occasion that one turns up and starts roaming around on the comparatively thickly populated island, the Icelanders usually feel that shooting it is the only sensible thing to do. On the other hand, no-one is allowed to kill a polar bear if it is at sea in Icelandic waters.

With the melting of the ice at a rapid pace, the polar bears have started moving toward the south in Greenland, which has meant some animals have had to be killed, Iceland-style, because of the threat to humans. It is not unheard of, although frustrating to the locals, that sled dogs have also been attacked and eaten by polar bears in search of food.

Since 1972 the World Wildlife Fund has had support and educational programs in place across the Arctic to try and protect not only the populations of the polar bear but their habitats as well. One worrying factor has been the amount of pesticide residues found in the bloodstream of many of the Arctic polar bears. It is because of issues like this, as well as earlier 'sport'-hunting before the 1973 agreement, that polar bears have been listed as vulnerable, with some areas showing a definite decline in already-modest numbers.

I came across some information about the harvesting of Polar Bears in Russia for the fur trade in the 1700s, with some estimates of 300 bears per year. It got me interested and I made a note to keep a look out for information on the species in other countries I visited.

It was strange to me that these animals that Westerners held in such high regard were also the main food staples of the people. In that sense it was a culture shock!

The people still seem to be able to maintain their own unique cultures and social customs. The Inuit and the Danish cultures are distinct of course, and yet the two have blended over time to create another individual Greenlandic culture. I saw variations of this culture in the different regions. Narsaq was different to Nuuk and different again in Ilulissat. I expected it would be different even further north. Greenland is the largest island in the world and yet also one of the most sparsely populated, as is most of the Arctic. The entire population of Greenland is well under 60,000. I found it amazing to travel to all these so-called main cities to find but a mere smattering of people living there.

At Narsarsuaq, I found that there was a botanical garden! I wouldn't have thought there could be such a thing as an Arctic botanical garden before I came to Greenland: but there was. It's called the Greenlandic Arboretum, and it's a place where locals are cultivating a collection of plants from the whole of the Arctic, not just Greenland.

I decided that while I was in Narsaq I would book into a hotel, and I found that the accommodation was more limited here than in Nuuk. I decided to book one night at a time in case my plans changed – and I was glad that I did. For, I was still working and needed a reliable internet connection. I was trying to secure a house purchase in Queenstown, New Zealand, which ended up being quite an ordeal! The lawyer I had decided that because I was overseas, he would try and charge me for things he hadn't done like obtaining reports and titles, which I actually ended up sorting out myself from Greenland. Note to self – never again.

For more, see:

> a-maverick.com/blog/southwest-greenland

CHAPTER 10

Roaming to Igaliku

I MET the owners of a hotel in Igaliku, and a group of their friends, while I was in the hotel at Narsaq. They were all very welcoming and I ended up getting on with them really well. There was Claus, Heidi, Jacques and his partner. They all hailed from different parts of Europe, Norway, Finland, France, Iceland and Denmark – and then throw a little New Zealand into the mix and we were quite a team! Jacques invited me to come and help them prepare the hotel for a big event. They were working in town that day but the following day they would take me through the Tunulliarfik Fjord and then on to their country hotel in Igaliku.

I was glad for the opportunity to get out and about with some company. There were two options to get to Igaliku. The first was to get a boat, and the second was to get a boat partway and then tramp (that is, hike; in New Zealand we say tramp) the rest of the way to the small settlement. Well, I chose tramping of course! Jacques told me that the tramp would be about six hours through snow and rock.

The big event they were hosting at their hotel was a conference where one hundred or so corporate clients were staying for four days. I remember wondering, why? How out of the way is that?

The tramp over to Igaliku turned out to be pretty easy actually, and I managed to carry all my stuff in my backpack without hassle.

Narsaq to Igaliku

Narsaq to Igaliku. The little red building is the hotel run by Jacques and his friends.

The scenery was fantastic and like nothing I had experienced before. What had seemed like harsh and unforgiving terrain from the plane window turned out to be some of the most beautiful landscape I had seen. When I arrived in Igaliku the reason for the corporate event's choice of location became very clear. Igaliku was beautiful!

I offered to help them prepare for the big corporate event. I'm not much of a cook so I offered to help shovel snow from around the van, so it could get out to collect the groups from the airport. There was a small tractor that needed to be started up too, so I helped with that. I remember some of the guys trying to haul in the buoy which had been left out at sea over the winter and drifted quite far out. It became a source of entertainment for us all watching them try to get it back closer to shore.

While I was there, I got talking to the people who worked in the hotel. They were all based in Narsarsuaq and they told me how hard the winters were there. I found it funny because they referred to Igaliku as being a farming community. There were sparse tufts of alpine grasses, but nothing like the rolling green hills of New Zealand's farming country.

The weather was amazing. Most days were overcast and grey, but on other days the sun popped out for a brief moment. There are times of the year when there is no sun at all and other times when the sun never sleeps. Two complete contrasts – I don't know how people lived here during the depths of winter when everything was hidden in darkness. I headed back into Narsaq and stayed in a hotel that only cost me US $100 a night with breakfast and lunch included. Great value for money, I say! I spent a lot of time wandering around, and I'm pretty sure I met most of the 167 residents that called Narsaq home.

I met the local chief, who also used to be Greenland's foreign minister. He was an environmentalist and was fighting uranium mining near Narsaq. When he learned that I was from New Zealand he told me he had met the prominent South Island Māori leader and first board chairman of the Sealord fishing company, Tipene O'Regan.

I told him about our problems with overfishing courtesy of firms like Sealord, to whom the Māori had granted fishing rights in return for a 50% shareholding in a deal brokered by the New Zealand government, which was supposed to lead to Māori economic development. Originally the idea was that this would provide Māori employment, but Sealord chartered internationally owned ships with their own crews.

I thought that was silly. Why didn't the Māori keep the jobs for themselves, and own their own ships? But that would have probably implied more of a long-term commitment than was possible under the current New Zealand fisheries management system, which was basically an extractive free-for-all, with several species being fished to the point of commercial extinction in New Zealand waters and not much being done about it despite numerous reports and media stories.

Since the 1980s, New Zealand had had a world-leading system of fisheries management on paper. The problem was that it did, indeed, exist mainly 'on paper', with few inspectors and unreported catches reliably thought to outweigh the catches that were reported. If Sealord didn't go hard-out to catch the last fish with international ships and crews, ships and crews that were hired short-term with no strings attached, free to go somewhere else once the New Zealand fishery started to falter, somebody else would.

Such were the perils of indigenous economic development schemes if ground-rules for sustainability were not strictly laid out and enforced. And the lessons were as relevant to Greenland as to anywhere else.

The Greenlandic people were quite knowledgeable about New Zealanders. Apparently, there had been a few of us visiting Greenland as of late. I remembered seeing an article in one of the New Zealand's newspapers about 22-year-old twins from Hamilton, south of Auckland, who planned to ski across Greenland's four major ice caps in 2014.

Over the next five days I was to find out a lot about Greenland from the locals. One of the women in the group I had met, Heidi, was originally from Iceland. She had lived in Greenland for almost 40 years and loved the Northern winters. She told me she hadn't liked the nearly perpetual darkness of winter at first but had become accustomed to it and had grown to love the northern winters over time. She told me that walruses and seals are caught on the temporary winter ice surrounding Narsaq at that time of year. The winter catch gets divided up and shared out amongst all the villagers. I thought that was quite traditional, and a brilliant display of community in a place where most people would find it hard to live. I also found it interesting that they didn't depend on the use of money so much: a slab of meat counted as payment for many things. Heidi told me that most of Greenland used to be like this until about twenty years ago, particularly in more northern places like Nuuk.

Jacques had been there for quite some years too; about thirty. He was from a place called Gap in France that sits by the border of Italy. He made a trip to Greenland out of curiosity and immediately fell in love with the place. He went and packed his things and moved there. The only qualm he had with Greenland is that they only had two or three months to make their annual income. So, the remaining 10 months of the year was spent exploring and just spending time with the people in the village. He actually owned a few businesses in Narsaq and surrounds: the Blue Ice café, the hostel in Narsaq, and the Country Hotel in Igaliku. On top of that though he also had boats for transporting tourists to Igaliku and around the fjords and hired out cabins as well, so he was quite the businessman.

Claus was from Denmark and had about five boats which he used for charters during the summer months. He said that the summer months ran from June to mid-September but that there was no guarantee of warmer weather even then. He reiterated to me that there was quite a bit of pressure during that time, as it was the only part of the year in which they could make money. Their earnings for the whole year really were booked up in the summer and that was that.

Of course, that's no different to running a skifield that makes its money in winter. But I suspect Greenland tourism is a bit more precarious. People have to come from quite a long way away, and it's a bit of an intrepid journey.

For more, see:

a-maverick.com/blog/roaming-igaliku

CHAPTER 11

Knud Rasmussen and the Origins of the Greenland Inuit

WHILE I was in Narsaq I heard plenty of the Greenlandic or Kalaallisut language being spoken. About 50,000 out of the 56,000 people in Greenland speak Greenlandic, which makes it the majority language and one of the most successfully preserved indigenous languages anywhere.

The Danish colonisers of Greenland made Kalaallisut into a written language in the 1700s and did not teach Danish in the state schools on the island until the 1920s.

A lot of research into the origins and culture of the Greenlandic people was done by Knud Rasmussen, a Danish man with an Inuit grandmother on his mother's side who was born in Jakobshavn, now Illulisaat. Rasmussen is famous as the leader of the Danish Literary Expedition, an epic journey across Greenland in which Rasmussen and his colleagues studied remote Inuit outposts and recorded their myths, tales and legends.

Knud Johan Victor Rasmussen, to record his full name, is very well known in Greenland and Denmark for his work with the Inuit. He sounded like quite the character – apparently, he had tried everything from acting to opera singing and eventually settled on becoming an anthropologist and explorer.

Rasmussen learned from the Inuit how to use a sled and train sledding dogs, setting out on his first expedition in 1902. He called his expeditions 'Thule' after the Greek word for the far north and set out to study the Inuit not just in Greenland but across Canada too. He had wanted to travel across Russia as well but in the early Bolshevik era, he wasn't able to get a visa. He collected many artefacts on his travels, wrote books and gave lectures about the Inuit people, contributing to the understanding of their cultures.

There is a museum dedicated to Rasmussen's memory in Ilulissat. Its exhibits are displayed inside the house in which he was born. Tickets to this museum also give access to the Ilulissat Art Museum, which I talk about a couple of chapters further on.

The Knud Rasmussen Museum, Ilulissat. Photograph by 'Makemake', August 2006, CC BY-SA 3.0, via Wikimedia Commons.

For more, see:

a-maverick.com/blog/knud-rasmussen

CHAPTER 12

The Regular but Intrepid Voyage of the Sarfaq Ittuk

Arctic Umiaq Line ports of call of the Sarfaq Ittuk

Wikimedia Commons map (2009) by Algkalv, public domain image (current on Wikipedia as of 6 October 2018)

I HAD thoroughly enjoyed my time in Narsaq, but it was time for me to see more of Greenland. There was a ship named the Sarfaq Ittuk, the only coastal ferry in Greenland. It was soon departing from Narsaq, and I booked a ticket to be on it. I've reproduced a stylised map of its route and ports of call just above; this is still current as of the time of writing, September 2021.

I had a few final errands to run while I was in town, I had to go to the local police station to get them to sign off on my identity for one of the final mortgage documents for the house I was buying in Queenstown, New Zealand.

That ended up being a big deal. Between the language barriers and cultural confusion, I almost got arrested for having two passports. Nobody'd told the local cops that many New Zealanders are entitled to hold a British EU passport as well as a Kiwi one, for old-timey Imperial reasons that aren't too different to the relationship between Greenland and Denmark.

Not knowing all this, they must have thought I was a British crook laundering the swag through the NZ property market while escaping to what I had no doubt mistakenly thought to be the sunny Greenland Riviera. In the end we managed to sort out the mix-up, and I got the documents away. I was not going to go through that again.

And so, I headed back to the hostel Jacques ran, where I had ended up staying in the end, and saw this big sale on the way back. Seal skins were on sale for just 30 Kroner or a bit over four dollars US. I wasn't overly impressed because I knew there had been restrictions imposed by the European Union to avoid the over-hunting of seals.

Should the pelts be on sale, or was that not a bit like ivory? Then again, the low price suggested that you couldn't take them out of the country. Maybe it was a purely local thing.

I was looking forward to the boat trip that would take me north past Nuuk to Knut Rasmussen's old birthplace of Ilulissat, or Jakobshavn. I said goodbye to everyone that I had met and thanked them so much for having me there in Narsaq – it had really been an adventure.

I made my way to the ferry terminal quite early in the morning and looked up to see the magnificent vessel I would be travelling on, the *Sarfaq Ittuk*. Well, it didn't look fancy and was nothing like the cruise ships we get down our coastlines in New Zealand, but I found it great all the same. The ship had been built in 2006 and was specially created to plough through water laden with icebergs. It can hold 249 people and has 52 cabins onboard.

This ship would be my oceangoing home for the next four nights and I was looking forward to seeing inside it! Once on board I was shown to my room which had a window that overlooked the Greenland Sea. So, you wouldn't even have to leave your room for views of icebergs and ocean if you didn't want to! I was really hoping to see seals and whales, and having that window gave me every opportunity to be staring out to sea. The rooms were very simple but cosy enough. The rocking of the ship was very gentle, and I had no trouble drifting off to sleep at night.

Leaving Narsaq, we sailed quite smoothly eastward to Qaqortoq before turning westward on the main journey. And alongside us rose the rugged peaks and mountains of the fjords.

Sarfaq Ittuk cruise: Day One

It was totally picturesque and when I wasn't roaming around or sipping hot coffee at the café, I could be found clicking away with my camera on the main deck.

The ship was full of all sorts of characters, and I met plenty of them in the café. I met a Norwegian guy who was in charge of oil clean-ups along the coast, a Russian engineer, a man named Leo from Korea, and an Inuit woman and her daughter. The Inuit woman told me she worked for a power company but stayed in a place called Sisimiut, a town midway between Nuuk and Ilulissat when she wasn't at work. She told me they often travelled on the ferry, and it had become a common mode of transport for the locals because the weather was so changeable and that affected the flights. She told me about how her parents had both passed away and she was dealing with a skin condition. I felt sorry for her; we had a good many conversations.

I also met a group of nurses from Denmark who were working in and around Greenland doing volunteer work – they were interesting! They found it a real culture shock working in such remote villages and the only way you could get to them was by a snowmobile or dog sled.

On board along the passageways there were all these information boards with species of animals like whales found in the Greenland Sea and maps of the route we would be taking.

I was amazed, when I looked at the map, at how close to Canada Greenland gets at its nearest point: 26 km to be exact! I'd thought of Greenland as being part of Europe more or less, with Iceland not really all that far from Norway and Greenland not really all that far from Iceland; but in the very high latitudes of the North Atlantic, everything sort-of squeezes together. That's precisely why the Vikings were able to make it all the way to Canada in their open longboats. They didn't need to be out of sight of land for as long as Columbus's sailors a few centuries later, mariners who took a more southerly route.

Day Two aboard the Sarfaq Ittuk

In a port, day two on the Sarfaq Ittuk.

The captain and the staff on board were great, and very informative! We started seeing massive icebergs on day two of the trip. The captain and everyone kept me informed and pointed out icebergs to me all the time. Although, I'm sure that they were so used to seeing them that they probably laughed at my excitement in seeing them! The Russian engineer was always out on the deck taking photos. He would be out there for hours and hours – the whole day. It was funny because he lived and worked in Nuuk and saw this a lot – but still he found the scenery amazing. We would talk for hours about our love of travel, and I was often standing right alongside him taking photographs.

Our first westbound port stop was Arsuk, which we arrived at on the same day we left Narsaq and Qaqortoq. I was told the name Arsuk meant 'beloved place' and had been the site of first a Norse settlement and then the Thule people.

Getting back out to sea was exciting though, and the further north we travelled the more icebergs we saw. I mean the icebergs were wondrous. Incredible. Amazing. I can't begin to describe them. Some were so huge they towered above the ferry, but we never got too close to those ones. They were further out to sea. I was so fascinated I just snapped photos the whole time, I'm surprised my face didn't get frozen to my camera. Most of the larger ones were out to sea, but others appeared surprisingly close. They made strange sounds as we passed them by, the ocean slapping at them, the creaking as they eased through the water and the eerie shrills as the wind blew past.

Iceberg

That's one of the main reasons I came to Greenland: to see ice and all the different kinds there were. The captain told me about how dangerous the ice could be. There were different types you have to watch out for and be wary of: glacier ice, ice caps, sea ice and icebergs were all different and each required different levels of caution. I didn't feel scared or worried, I felt completely at ease under the company and charge of the captain. He had been sailing this stretch of ocean for a long time now and I trusted his judgement. I admired them all. You had to be a bloody good captain to sail through this ocean for so long, so he knew his stuff alright.

Iceberg

Another port further north, after Nuuk, was Maniitsoq. It's the sixth largest town in Greenland and was once a major reindeer trading post in the 19th Century. Maniitsoq also had a few archaeological sites that dated back over four thousand years. It was really very similar to the other port towns along the way a mere smattering of houses, rock and snow. The captain pointed out that there were only roughly 2,200 residents and it was a town whose population was always declining because people just couldn't find enough work.

We were on our way to the last stop, twelve hours before we arrived in Ilulissat, at a port at the southern end of Disko Bay called Aasiaat.

It was always exciting docking at a port because everybody came out to wave at you and greet the disembarking passengers. People said that Aasiaat was the best place to spot whales and seals along the western coastline. And that seemed to be true as far as seals went. Out on the water, on small icebergs, were thick brown slugs which I soon saw to be seals. Their heads would bob out of the water every now and then and when the ferry got too close to the icebergs they were resting on, they would dive over the side and disappear into the grey water. I spent much of that day hoping to see a whale of some sort, but I didn't in the end. I was a bit disappointed, but at least I had got to read the sign in on the ship that told me all about them!

The issues surrounding whale hunting were another interesting affair. The Whaling Commission allows families to hunt whales to feed their families and villages but there has been a rise in commercial whaling alongside this – which was a cause for slight concern. Whales and the Inuit and Greenlandic culture are so closely linked with history and tradition it would be unimaginable for them to be without whale hunting. The common belief is that every Greenlandic person should have access to whale meat – it is just a way of life. In 2014, Greenland statistics showed that 176 large whales were caught as traditional food. Of the total, 157 were minke whales, twelve fin whales and seven humpback whales.

International wildlife organisations have tried to get Greenlandic people to sign a contract with a restriction on the number of whales caught per year. It wasn't taken too kindly by Greenlandic people and yet in Denmark whaling is illegal. The Arctic whales that are most commonly caught for food are the bowhead, minke, humpback, fin, beluga and narwhal. I was really hoping to see a narwhal; more like a dolphin then a whale, it is quite small, and the male has a twisted horn at the front. I didn't though, and maybe that was another sign of global warming.

We had a short stop in Aasiaat. A few people disembarked. A few people boarded. And then we were off again. It was as we were heading back into the deep ocean that we almost got stranded.

It was probably the only time I did get a bit panicked. There was more and more ice appearing in the water and it was thicker and bigger than before. The ferry started to creak and was barely moving through the ocean.

The captain was pretty calm, though, and told us not to worry. So, I didn't. It would be a great story to tell everyone back home and, oh, also for a book, right?

Aasiaat, with Hotel Sømandshjemmet (The Seaman's Home Hotel)

Leo was from South Korea and had excellent English. He loved travelling and had already been to many countries even though he was only in his early twenties. We got on really well, and he was telling me that he had booked a place to stay in Ilulissat on hostel.com. It was only US $50 a night and it turned out it was with a local family. We finally arrived in Ilulissat and I was quite excited to be there. I'd heard there were heaps of walking trails in the area and plenty of historical museums. A few more touristy things to do than in Narsaq, I'd think.

By this time, we had come about 1,300 kilometres, or roughly the same as the distance from the northern tip of the North Island of New Zealand to the southern tip of the South Island as the jet flies. Narsaq and Ilulissat weren't that far apart on the same basis, more like about 900 km, but we'd had to sail round a convex coast and stop off at whole lot of places, making more distance. 900 kilometres or 1,300, it still didn't look very far when plotted on a map of the whole of Greenland!

With around 4,000 permanent residents, Ilulissat was quite a bit larger than Narsaq and a fair bit busier. Ilulissat is also known as the birthplace of icebergs! To the south-east of the town there was a UNESCO world heritage site in the form of the Ilulissat Icefjord – which I will have a quite a lot more to say about, a little further on.

Like Nuuk, Ilulissat is made up of an old city and a new city – although I still wouldn't call it a 'city', it made for a very interesting contrast to Nuuk and to Narsaq. You could be walking up a hill to the Arctic hotel even and get sweeping views out sea and to the icebergs. It was in a much wilder location than Nuuk, or Narsaq. It just seemed like a dream, despite the biting cold winds that would give your face a slap around.

Leo and I decided we'd explore Ilulissat together so when the driver came to collect him from the ferry terminal, Leo told him I was looking for a room to stay. They dropped me off at the Arctic Hotel, which I didn't really fancy so I thought I'd try my luck with a hostel like Leo had. I wound up in the home of Mona and Hans, who agreed they could house me for the eight days I had planned to be in Ilulissat. Mona and Hans were great! They sat down and endured all the questions about life in Greenland. What did they eat, did they ever eat polar bear, what about whales etc etc?

Mona told me more about the traditional boots the women wore made of seal skins. They are called Kamiks and every Greenlandic woman owns a pair, they are a very precious item and cost a fortune to buy in a shop. She told me she had seen some for sale at the equivalent of US $600. They come above the knee to help keep out the wet snow and ice and there was room to tuck your trousers in, another layer of insulation against the cold. Traditionally they painted them but in modern times they use embroidery and beads as embellishments.

For more, see:

a-maverick.com/blog/sarfaq-ittuk

CHAPTER 13

Ilulissat and the Huskies – And Greenland's biggest Glacier that isn't there anymore

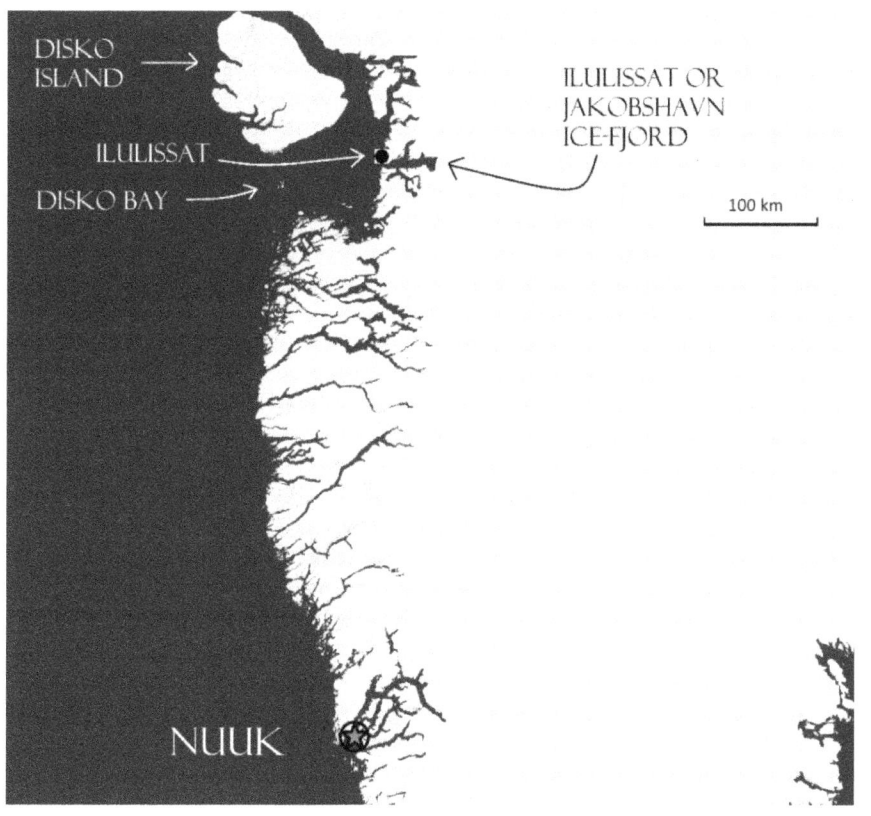

The Ilulissat area, in relation to Nuuk. The wide fiord formerly occupied until recently by the Jakobshavn Glacier lies just north of Ilulissat.

I LOVED exploring Ilulissat, which I thought was a very quaint little town. Blanketed in patches of ice and snow, it was positioned on a slight incline with stunning views out to sea.

I managed to rope Leo into visiting the Ilulissat Art Museum with me. Most of the pictures' theme was – you guessed it – ice! There were some stunning images and scenes portrayed by many Greenland artists. It didn't seem to matter if most of their world was grey, they were very skilled at getting the whitish blue colour of ice perfect. A museum we visited gave a good look at Greenland's history. This was, of course, Knud Rasmussen's Museum. It was contained in the house he had been born in, and there was a statue of Ilulissat's most famous citizen outside. There were also lots of preserved boats of various kinds, and the hunting and fishing equipment the Inuit traditionally used. It was quite a cultural eye-opener to see all that, and so was the house itself. I have been to so many different museums all over the world and I make a point of visiting them wherever I go. Sometimes the little ones are just as intriguing as the big ones.

Leo and I spent a lot of time just exploring Ilulissat – we also found the little church, Zion's Church, perched right on the waterfront. It was funny and amazing to see a church with icebergs casually floating in the water behind it. I have never seen anything like it.

Leo and I went and did a few of the walks and trails around Ilulissat and found some great areas where we took a few photographs. We made our way to a part of the UNESCO World Heritage site – the so-called Ilulissat or Jakobshavn Icefjord, the maker the maker of some of the biggest icebergs in the world. The icefjord (also spelt ice fjord, or icefjord) is so named because it is a fjord full of floating icebergs.

The present icefjord was completely occupied, as recently as the mid-nineteenth century, by a huge glacier called the Jakobshavn Glacier, which has since melted almost completely (more on this remarkable development below!) The smaller glaciers that used to feed the Jakobshavn Glacier now fill the icefjord with icebergs instead. In winter, the icefjord also freezes over on top. When I was there, the winter ice was just about to melt. It was still strong enough to go dog sledding on top, but my dog sledding trip would be one of the last ones of the season.

It was a few hours' hike; although it wasn't really what I would class as a hike apart from all the rocks and rough arctic grasses we had to scramble over. Eventually we found ourselves on a wooden boardwalk over the more sensitive grass-type plants. Another thumbs-up to Greenland for being so environmentally conscious – I heard that the Greenlanders were early adopters of the nature boardwalk idea.

All around Ilulissat there are paths leading to the massive icefjord, and Leo and I just sat on the picnic table watching the ice move around in the water. It was so peaceful. We had expected other tourists, but we were the only people there! What made my jaw drop was the sheer size of the things: these icebergs were monstrous! Just massive walls of ice that towered into the sky. Their low rumblings and sounds of cracking ice were magical. We sat there in silence for an hour or two just watching and listening to everything.

It felt really like a dream: I couldn't believe I was here. I had travelled nearly twenty thousand kilometres across the globe to lay my eyes on the world's most productive icefjord.

Ilulissat: Huskies, Zion's Church, the western sea, and the great Ilulissat Icefjord

Ilulissat with art and the Art Museum

Ilulissat

It wasn't bleak, dull or boring here either – it was spectacular even with the lack of greenery. That was made up for in the deep green and grey of the ocean and the sparkling ice. The tundra and alpine grasses and shrubs were even soft hues of yellow and brown. In fact, it really was mesmerising and beautifully peaceful. Leo and I returned to town, and we just gushed at how incredible the whole thing was, and how glad we were to have done it!

Back in town, we went back to my hostel for a cup of coffee. We got talking about making a more serious tour of the icefjord, which penetrates a long way inland and was fed by a colossal glacier variously known as the Jakobshavn Glacier, the Jakobshavn Isbræ (which means Jakobshavn Glacier in Danish), the Jakobshavn Isbræ Glacier (which repeats itself), Sermeq Kujalleq (Southern Glacier in Kalaalissut Inuit, Southern in the sense of just south of Ilulissat), and the Ilulissat Glacier. This was perhaps the most studied glacier in the world and was generally known worldwide as the Jakobshavn Glacier, so I will stick to that name while using the indigenous name for the town, Ilulissat. As to why I keep saying "was," well, I'll get to that in a moment.

The ice-streams that feed into the icefjord are altogether the most productive in Greenland and perhaps in the Northern Hemisphere, calving possibly as much as 46 cubic kilometres of icebergs a year, or about 40 billion tonnes of ice, into the icefjord, which is about a kilometre deep for most of its length but with a shallower sill, about 300 metres deep, at its mouth. This is a very common depth profile for fiords (or fjords) that used to contain glaciers; the fiords in south-western New Zealand are similar. The glacier excavates the fiord to a kilometre in depth, but the scraping effect is weaker near the end, where rocks actually pile up (the terminal moraine).

In the Ilulissat Icefjord the icebergs, themselves up to a kilometre tall, float down from the Greenland icecap until they get to the entrance near Ilulissat and pile up, grinding and groaning and being smashed into by newer bergs, until they break down into smaller bergs and get pushed over the sill.

The Jakobshavn Glacier used to occupy the whole of the icefjord, calving its bergs directly into the open sea. The glacier was regularly monitored by scientists from 1851 onwards, which is why I say it was one of the best-studied in the world. In 1851 the Jakobshavn Glacier presented the striking sight of a tongue of ice running like a giant frozen river across 50 km of open country from the inland icecap to the shore. It lay in the trench that the ice had carved for itself over millennia, the ice dropping off into the open sea when it hit the sill at the end.

Remarkably, what the scientists got there just in time to witness was the transformation of that river of solid ice into a finger of the sea extending 50 km inland from Ilulissat, with ice floating on top. In other words, the transformation of a large glacier into a large fiord: something that possibly hadn't happened anywhere since the end of the last ice age, and certainly hadn't been scientifically observed from start to finish.

Today, the Jakobshavn Glacier no longer exists as a single glacier. What now exists are the ice-streams that historically fed into it. These are the Kangia Glacier and the Dead Glacier.

With the Jakobshavn Glacier gone, the glaciers feeding the icefjord flow at something like twice the rate that they used to. It's a bit like removing a cork from a bottle. Although, even in the old days, the Jakobshavn Glacier was still probably the main source of icebergs in the

Northern Hemisphere, including (most probably) the one that sunk the *Titanic*.

It's thought that the icefjord, its bottom well below sea level, may penetrate all the way across Greenland, so that, hypothetically, the collapse of the ice sheet could continue all the way across, isolating the southern part of Greenland as a new island.

We looked at some of the tours to the remaining headwaters (head-ices?) of the former Jakobshavn Glacier, which meant travelling 50 km inland from Ilulissat. The cheapest we found was one for 1400 Kroner or US $150. It entitled us to a two-hour sledge ride to the glacier. There were quite a few companies offering different tour packages.

We thought about it for a bit and Leo decided he would go on a shorter tour while I decided that no I would go all out: because I am in Greenland for goodness's sake! So, I booked a tour with a company called Nature Tours that was managed by an Italian guy. The tour I booked meant I would spend the day travelling to the main area of the Ilulissat Icefjord and then spend the night in a hut there, where we would get to do some ice fishing! I didn't mind fishing, though I wasn't keen on eating seal or seeing one killed. Then we would travel right up to the Kangia Glacier and the Dead Glacier (not the best name, I know).

At 11a.m. I met my guide, Yush, and his pack of twelve sled dogs at the meeting point to the south of the town. The trip was amazing: the way the dogs run harmoniously along the slippery ice, the way the sun glints off the bumpy surfaces and that feeling of flying across the ice. It was all just marvellous. I couldn't help but call out in the pure joy of the moment!

Yush was very friendly. He told me how he only feeds his dogs whale meat, seal and halibut. I could see that dogs were very well-trained. He said they were very well-behaved and listened to him most of the time! He would call out what sounded like "you-you" to them, and he explained to me that meant 'go on' 'go on'.

The trip to the hut would be a solid five hours of sled riding, though we would make a couple of stops along the way to let the dogs rest. The poor dogs had a bit of struggle getting up some of the hills, it was getting warmer, and the snow was melting in places. I'm pretty sure I was one of the last tours to the glaciers for that season before it got too warm, and the ice became thinner.

So, that was a quid pro quo for arriving too early to do the full summer hikes!

The wind was icy, and it battered me full blast in the face. About an hour into the trip, I was putting on another layer of gloves over the insulated ones I already had on, it was getting colder the closer we got. We arrived at the hut at about 4 p.m. Yush helped me unload my pack and take it into the hut. I watched him from the window as he settled the dogs and fed them. I was amazed at how sleek their bodies were, all the fatty meat they had to eat and yet there wasn't an inch of fat on them. Although it was pretty hard to see much beyond all their fluff!

Yush told me sometimes he did have to whip them sometimes when they didn't do what they were told and tried to stray from the path. It was only because the ice was thinning and there was always the possibility of them running onto a soft spot and going through the ice. Still, I felt a bit sorry for them. They worked very hard, those dogs.

Ilulissat

Dog Sledding, Ilulissat Icefjord

What happens if you take your sunglasses off. The photo doesn't really capture the glare. The Inuit used sunglasses made with little slits in them. And here is a picture of Yush in camp at the end of the day!

Yush made me salmon and rice for dinner. It was the beginning of summer and so the sun was in the sky for 24 hours, or nearly so. Even

when the summer sun does go below the horizon in these latitudes, it's more of a brief onset of twilight around midnight after which the sun pops up again. It felt weird eating a late evening meal in what still seemed to be broad daylight.

We put the heaters on and got the beds ready. I needed to go to the toilet and there was none in the hut, so I went for a little wander and to my surprise could make out the huge spikes of ice from the Kangia Glacier in the distance. At night I could hear the glaciers moving; it was unreal and really loud!

I woke in the morning and started packing. I could hear the dogs were having a tussle outside. Yush said that usually the others will try and have a go at the lead dog: they all want to be pack leader but only the toughest is. I noticed that Yush's lead dog was much larger than the rest and I thought the other dogs must be pretty brave to try and take him on.

The history of dog sledding is quite interesting. The Alaskan husky is the most common breed used to pull sleds, or sledges or sleighs, which all mean pretty much the same thing as far as I can tell. The final refinement of dogs bred for that exact purpose, the Alaskan husky became a recognised breed in the 1800s. Beyond being a most enjoyable sport and the highlight of my trip, dogsledding was for a long time a means of transport for the Inuit, a way to haul the fruit of hunting trips back to their outposts and villages.

Historians believe that the ancestors of huskies were brought from Mongolia during the original migrations to the Arctic. However, for a long time they were just dogs. The development of practical dog sleds is associated with the Thule culture, which also perfected the kayak and the

Inuit version of the toggle harpoon, a hard-to-pull-out design used by several indigenous whaling cultures. Thereafter, dog sleds became an important means of transport wherever the Inuit lived.

Europeans and Inuit used dog sleds for exploration of Arctic areas. Well-funded expeditions also took this traditional form of transport to the opposite pole, in Antarctica.

Another husky-like breed called malamute was also developed in the 1800s. This was like a husky but stronger and stockier. The malamute was used to pull wood from lumber mills.

Dog sleds were the deliverers of mail and other essentials across icy landscapes in the 1800s and 1900s before the development of more motorised methods of transport. Dog trails have been formally established in regions where horses and trains cannot reach. And most famously of all perhaps, there is the example of the January 1925 mercy dash in which a dog team delivered medical serum to Nome, Alaska to stem an epidemic when nothing else could get through the winter dark and biting cold; an event commemorated each year in that state's famous Iditarod dog sled race.

Anyway, in Greenland the dogs that pull the sleds are simply known as 'Greenlandic huskies' or 'Greenlandic dogs' – they looked like huskies to me!

We left by about ten in the morning: although, really, I had no physical sense of what time it was. After we left, it was just a short, one-hour trip to get to the Kangia glacier. Yush got me right up close, which was just magic, and I got a heap of photos! Yush said that by late June the whole area would turn into open water. I found that hard to believe looking at all the snow everywhere, as if it lay on solid ground.

The Kangia Glacier with cracks in the frozen sea of the Ilulissat Icefjord. It was getting toward the end of the sledding season when this picture was taken, and the fjord would soon be open sea.

The ride to the glacier was smooth and felt quick! The dogs pulled with ease over the snowy ground, ropes attached to each harness and held tightly by Yush. There were six dogs either side with the same two dogs at the front. We got within ten metres of the glacier and the dogs got a bit stuck in some snow. It was beginning to melt so we couldn't go any further. I got off and let Yush attend to the dogs and to getting the sled unstuck from the snow. I could see the huge ice cap moving and shifting. The sounds of ice splitting and crashing into the water echoed around the vast landscapes. It was beautiful – epic even. I got some amazing photos of the Kangia glacier and the ice cap.

We continued on to see if we could get close to the other glacier, the Dead Glacier, where the Inuit go fishing. We saw men with guns hunting for seals. They called out greetings to us as we passed by. I could see they were having trouble with their dog sled teams too. In places, the ice had water across the top, making it tricky. It was a Thursday, and that seemed to be the local day for hunting and fishing as there were quite a few people around. They had snowmobiles or twenty-dog sled teams that covered more ground at a faster pace than we could.

Yush decided it would be too dangerous to try to get any closer, so we reluctantly headed back to Ilulissat. The views were amazing and if we had gone under the water at that moment, I would have died a very happy woman. Yush was very apologetic the whole way back that we didn't get to the second glacier or that I didn't get to see the men fishing. I told him not to worry: the scenery and experience had been enough and at the very least I had seen the Kangia glacier.

Seeing Yush's relationship with his dog sled team was fascinating, and I told him I had learned so much from our short trip. I had seen glaciers in New Zealand, France, Pakistan and Nepal, yet I was still amazed by the Kangia Glacier. Yush told me on the way back to Ilulissat that using dog sleds was becoming more unusual in modern times. People now used snowmobiles or helicopters in preference to the traditional dog sleds.

But of course, these modern (in)conveniences are horrible noisy things: not the same as dashing through the snow in a sleigh pulled by eager animals. Maybe in the future people will have electric transport charged by the perpetual sunshine, and that will be closer to the old experience.

On return to Ilulissat I caught up with Leo and told him about my journey. He was a bit jealous he didn't come in the end. I went back to my hostel at Hans and Mona's, where they were cooking dinner. It was my last night in Ilulissat before I returned to Nuuk to catch a flight to Iceland, and they wanted to cook something special.

To my shock they were cooking seal meat. It was something I had made a conscious effort not to eat; it just didn't sit right with me. In New Zealand, seals are heavily protected by the Department of Conservation (DOC) and I had been a uniformed volunteer DOC ranger myself, so you can see the conflict. Not to mention the fact that seals look a lot like dogs, to which they are in fact related, with their big faithful brown eyes!

But of course, I couldn't really tell Hans and Mona I wasn't going to eat their wonderful seal meal. So, I sat down at the table with them, and they dished me a big portion of suaasat, a traditional soup. It is a very simple soup with onion, potatoes and sometimes other vegetables and always with seal meat or another marine mammal.

This time it was made with seal meat, maybe a harp seal. It was very different, quite unlike any meat I had ever seen before. It was a deep reddish brown and very oily.

Like all animals that have red meat, seals store up oxygen in their muscles in a red compound, much the same as the red substance in blood, to give them more endurance. The more an animal is likely to go into what athletes call 'oxygen debt', the darker and redder its meat. You even see this with fast-swimming fish, which is why tuna steaks are red. The meat of marine mammals that need to make deep dives, such as seals and whales, is incredibly dark.

I had expected the seal meat to taste fishy, but it didn't at all. I was thankful, though, that it wasn't whale meat. I don't think I could have brought myself to eat that!

The nineteen days I had spent exploring Greenland had been fantastic! I had found it quite expensive, but because of its remote location that was understandable. The further north you travelled the more expensive it got; the cost of transporting items really accounted for the high prices. I found out that most of the produce is flown in from Denmark, which only adds to the premium.

A few families told me that their children went to Denmark to make more money to pay for things. Often, this migration was seasonal. The Greenland winters were a time of temporary unemployment in many local occupations, especially the ones that depended on tourism. It was actually quite good for young people to get away at that time of year.

The only downer on my trip was learning and seeing the effects of pollution and overfishing. Some fish species were near extinction because of commercial fishing, and some whale species had been close to extinction before whaling was banned as well. I also got an insight to the

Inuit people's way of life, and how they were viewed within their own country. In Greenland where the Inuit are the majority it isn't too bad, but in Denmark I saw they were treated quite badly as so many minority groups in the world are.

As for the staple foods in Greenland, these really are anything related to the sea, plus caribou (wild reindeer) in places that are temperate enough for caribou to graze. All marine animals are eaten everywhere: seal, seabirds, whale and fish. It is cheaper and probably more wholesome, overall, than buying expensive shop goods.

(From Greenland to Polynesia, shop goods such as sugary soft drinks and fatty corned beef are often blamed for the deteriorating health of indigenous peoples, who seem to be healthier when leading a traditional lifestyle. Marine mammals contain a lot of fat, too. But it's the healthy Omega-3 kind, as in the fish.)

Greenlanders rely most heavily on the proceeds of hunting and fishing in winter, when the shipping of supplies becomes more difficult and when the freezing weather preserves locally caught meat and fish naturally in any case.

I would have liked to have gone north beyond Ilulissat, but it was going to cost me at least another US $1,000 to go any further. I hadn't realised it would cost so much to go beyond the end of the regular ferry service, until I got there and explored my options. But that's OK – there is always next time!

I had loved every minute of it, and the chance to see glaciers and meet the local people had been even better. Learning about the history and traditions of the Inuit had been the icing on the cake!

For more, see:

a-maverick.com/blog/ilulissat-huskies

Conclusion, and Epilogue

I GREATLY enjoyed my travels through the lands of the Inuit. I was amazed by the resourcefulness with which people could live so far north, in lands that I had assumed would be a frozen waste but were often green.

Since I was there, President Trump mused that he would like to buy Greenland. Ironically, this wasn't the first time the Americans have tried to take over the island, which has huge strategic significance for them. Back in the 1940s the Danes were offered $100 million for Greenland by President Truman's administration but refused to take it. The fact that Denmark then joined NATO meant that the Americans were stay on and eventually build and operate their still-operational Thule, or Pituffik, base in the far north without actually taking over the island.

There has also been a drive for full independence from Denmark, with most of the votes in the April 2021 elections going to pro-independence parties and candidates. On the other hand, the two main parties in the current legislature treat independence as a long-term goal, to be achieved once Greenland can stand on its own two feet economically, which they think will take at least another ten years. At present, Greenland gets a lot of money from the Danes in order to balance its budget. If. Greenland became independent too quickly and then had to look to the Americans for support instead, that would surely come with strings attached.

To finish, while I was in Ilulissat, I met some young Sámi, the indigenous peoples of European Scandinavia, who were on a cultural tour among the Inuit. That was fascinating, as I had only recently discovered that there were indigenous people in Scandinavia as well. That is a subject I talked about in my 2018 book *A Maverick Inuit Way and the Vikings*, and I might write about it some more in the future.

Acknowledgements and Thanks

THANKS to everyone who helped me to discover the lands of the North!

Additional praise is due to my editor Chris Harris, and to everyone who checked my manuscript along the way. Any errors that may remain, as always, are mine.

And thanks to you, for reading.

Other books by Mary Jane Walker

Did you like *Go Greenland?* If so, please leave a review!

And you may also like to have a look at the other books I've written, all of which have sales links on my website a-maverick.com.

A Maverick Traveller

A funny, interesting compilation of Mary Jane's adventures. Starting from her beginnings in travel it follows her through a life filled with exploration of cultures, mountains, histories and more.

A Maverick New Zealand Way

The forerunner of the present book, *A Maverick New Zealand Way* was a finalist in Travel at the International Book Awards, 2018.

A Maverick Cuban Way

Trek with Mary Jane to Fidel's revolutionary hideout in the Sierra Maestra. See where the world nearly ended and the Bay of Pigs and have coffee looking at the American Guantánamo Base, all the while doing a salsa to the Buena Vista Social Club.

A Maverick Pilgrim Way

Pilgrim trails are not just for the religious! Follow the winding ancient roads of pilgrims across the continent of Europe and the Mediterranean.

A Maverick USA Way

Mary Jane took Amtrak trains around America and visited Glacier, Yellowstone, Grand Teton, Rocky Mountain and Yosemite National Parks before the snow hit. She loved Detroit which is going back to being a park, and Galveston and Birmingham, Alabama.

A Maverick Himalayan Way

Mary Jane walked for ninety days and nights throughout the Himalayan region and Nepal, a part of the world loaded with adventures and discoveries of culture, the people, their religions and the beautiful landscapes.

A Maverick Inuit Way and the Vikings

Mary Jane's adventures in the Arctic take her dog sledding in Greenland, exploring glaciers and icebergs in Iceland, and meeting some interesting locals.

Iran: Make Love not War

Iran is not what you think. It's diverse, culturally rich, and women have more freedoms than you would imagine.

The Scottish Isles: Shetlands, Orkneys and Hebrides (Part 1)

In 2018, Mary Jane decided to tour the islands that lie off the coast of Scotland. She made it around the Orkney and Shetland groups, and to the inner-Hebrides islands of Raasay, Mull, Iona and Staffa as well. She was amazed to discover that Norse influences were as strong as Gaelic ones, indeed stronger on the Orkneys and Shetlands.

Catchy Cyprus: Once was the Island of Love

This is a short book based on Mary Jane's visit to Cyprus, the island that copper's named after and the legendary birthplace of Aphrodite, Greek goddess of love. A former British possession in the Mediterranean Sea, Cyprus is divided into Greek-dominated and Turkish-dominated regions with United Nations troops in between.

Lovely Lebanon: A Little Country with a Big History

"I visit the small country of Lebanon, north of Israel, a country whose name means 'the white' in Arabic because of its snow-capped mountains.

Lebanon is divided between Christian and Muslim communities and has a history of civil war and invasion. For all that, it is very historic, with lots of character packed into a small space."

Eternal Egypt: My Encounter with an Ancient Land

In this book, Mary Jane explores Egypt, a cradle of civilisation described by the ancient Greek historian Herodotus as the 'gift of the Nile'. Mary Jane put off going to Egypt for years before she finally went. She's glad she did: there's so much more to Egypt than the pyramids!

The Neglected North Island: New Zealand's other half

In this book Mary Jane explores New Zealand's less touristy North Island. *The Neglected North Island* was judged **'Best Antipodean Cultural Travel Book 2021' by** *Lux Life* **magazine** (lux-review.com) and is also a **2021 IPPY Awards Bronze medallist** in Australia/New Zealand/Pacific Rim – Best Regional Non-Fiction

The Sensational South Island: New Zealand's Mountain Land

In this book, which is the companion to *The Neglected North Island,* Mary Jane explores New Zealand's mountainous South Island. She branches out from obvious tourist traps like Queenstown to explore this large but thinly populated island's lesser-known byways, historic cities and diverse landscapes, which vary from subtropical jungles where the world's southernmost palm trees grow, to much chillier places that look like Iceland and Greenland and even like Mars.

A Nomad in Nepal

A Nomad in Nepal and the Lands Next Door updates Mary Jane's earlier book, *A Maverick Himalayan Way*. With links to blog posts containing colour photographs and videos, *A Nomad in Nepal and the Lands Next Door* describes Mary Jane's three trips, so far, to Nepal and the Himalayan region.

Delving deeply into Himalayan history, *A Nomad in Nepal* is also a mine of useful firsthand experience about guiding and trekking pitfalls and the politics of the region, all while describing epic treks in Nepal and visits to Sikkim, Dharamshala (Himachal Pradesh), Sringagar (Kashmir) and the exotic Chitral region of Pakistan as well, hard-up against Afghanistan, where the local Kalash tribe is menaced by the Taliban.

A Kiwi on the Amtrak Tracks

Kiwi adventurer Mary Jane Walker explored America by Amtrak Train, travelling one and a half times around the lower 48 states and stopping off in Hawai'i as well. *A Kiwi on the Amtrak Tracks* is the latest book by the author of the IPPY award-winning *The Neglected North Island: New Zealand's other half* and award finalists *A Maverick New Zealand Way* and *Iran: Make Love Not War*.

www.ingramcontent.com/pod-product-compliance
Lightning Source LLC
Chambersburg PA
CBHW022112090426
42743CB00008B/822